Praise for *Nature Knows*

"This is passionate writing, authorship at its best! You will come away from *Nature Knows* with a renewed sense of direction and calm, poetic insights into nature's engaging lessons, and a philosophy that is both appealing and practical. Rothwell vividly demonstrates how you can improve your life and accent your well-being with a fervent attention to the botanical world. Know that this book will change your thinking and change your attitude in so many beautiful ways. You will be awed. Guaranteed!"

-Anthony D. Fredericks, author of *The Healing Wisdom of the Forest: Timeless Lessons of Renewal, Tranquility, and Joy*

"This delightful book is an insightful guide that helps the reader reconnect with their Essential Nature using the wisdom of plants. Blending psychology, lived experience, and nature-based metaphor, this book offers a grounded framework for understanding belonging, energy, rest, boundaries, and growth. It reminds us that thriving in life is not about discovering what's wrong with us or fixing ourselves, but about finding the conditions where we can truly flourish and grow."

-Holly Worton, author of *If Trees Could Talk*

NATURE KNOWS

Grow and Thrive through the Wisdom of Plants

MARY ROTHWELL

Interior illustrations by Barbara G. Butz

For more information, email mary@maryrothwell.net.

ISBN: 979-8-90057-211-6 - Ebook

ISBN: 979-8-90057-212-3 - Paperback

ISBN: 979-8-90057-213-0 - Hardcover

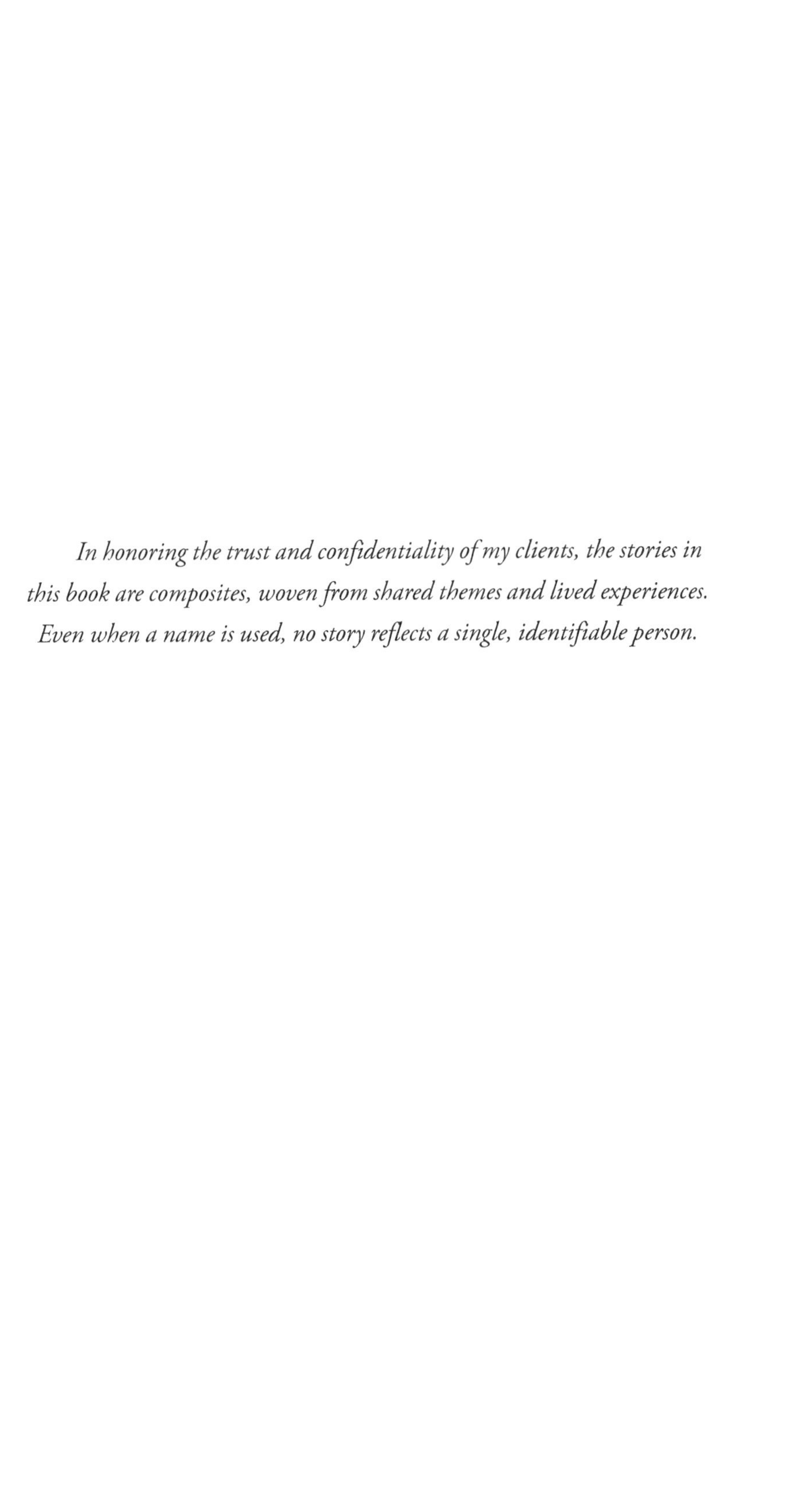

In honoring the trust and confidentiality of my clients, the stories in this book are composites, woven from shared themes and lived experiences. Even when a name is used, no story reflects a single, identifiable person.

BEYOND THESE PAGES

The belief at the heart of this book—that plants hold profound wisdom for how we grow, rest, adapt, and thrive—didn't stop at these pages. It inspired an entire podcast devoted to exploring those lessons through real women's lives and stories.

For centuries, the phrase *"shrinking violet"* has been used to diminish women, implying they were meant to be small or meek. Yet in nature, violets tell a very different story. They fold their flowers at night to rest, not retreat. They endure harsh conditions, return year after year, and play an essential role in the ecosystem.

My podcast *No Shrinking Violets* brings the themes of this book to life through conversations with women who embody resilience, wisdom, and unapologetic growth.

You can listen at maryrothwell.net/podcast
or wherever you get your podcasts.

For Julie ~

my fellow nature nerd, witchy wanderer, and truest friend.

You have the most beautiful heart.

CONTENTS

PREFACE

When I was a kid, I was drawn to nature. For hours, I would sit alone in the woods. I never thought about why I went there; it was instinctual. I could just exist there, among the trees and plants, birds and chattering squirrels. I grew to love the warm, musty scent of fallen leaves under my feet, the sparkle of dappled sun on the path, the rise and fall of birdsong. I felt safe there. Being in nature provided freedom from whatever pressures might push at the edges of that forest.

My tendency to find solitude through internal stillness when among people led my mom to label me "backward." As I matured, I mentally softened the word to "shy." And, finally, after reading *Quiet* by Susan Cain, I identified myself—with relief and a bit of smugness—as "introverted."

At 17, when it was time to choose a career path, I leaned toward floriculture (I didn't know something like *horticulture* existed), but when I realized most of the work involved weddings—thus, weekends—I chose to pursue an education degree, with the random logic of the young.

This decision likely protected me from losing my passion for flowers and, in time, plants themselves, because I didn't make it the source of my income. Instead, I combined my fascination with human nature and my knack for problem-solving into the nearly perfect vocation—counseling. Lord knows, I was observant, and I wanted a career that created change in the world. My experience has included work with clients of all ages—from elementary through high school, to community college, a satellite campus of a major land-grant university, and private practice. For many of those years, I also wore other hats and had roles in community education, outreach, and administration.

I loved my work. It felt like it mattered. And when my job role shifted or the climate of the working environment declined, I moved on. Each job change brought new challenges while still allowing me to use my natural instincts for connecting to people.

As for my love of nature, I continue to go to the woods to hike and contemplate. Spring still makes me feel like I will burst open like the earliest blooms of redbud (*Cercis candadensis*), *Forsythia*, *Crocus*, and aconite (*Eranthis hyemalis*).

Yet even for me, appreciating the beauty and value of *all* plants had a learning curve. In the same way we sometimes judge one another too quickly, appreciating the positive qualities of plants can require us to soften our assumptions and harsh judgments. I can ruefully admit that when I encountered coneflower (*Echinacea*) growing on the property of my first home, I took one look at those drooping petals and prickly stamen and promptly pulled it out. When I learned of its benefit as a native species, I paid money for new plants and replanted them. Gardening is a lesson in humbleness. And a reminder to keep an open mind.

Coneflower (Echinacea)

I eventually became certified as a Master Gardener so I could change the world through community education. I was co-owner of an organic fruit and vegetable farm and, at each property I owned, I planned and planted more and more evolved gardens, anchored by tough and beautiful native plants and more exotic perennials that I couldn't resist adding to the blueprint.

Each season increasingly revealed that plants and their growth could inform my work with people, as well as my own instinctive inner *knowing*. I began to realize how often I said variations of, "Like plants, we know, inside, what we really need." (My poor husband probably hears this in his sleep.) And I started to see plant habits and quirks as analogies for life situations and relationships. I began using these analogies in my therapy work, and I even created outreach for college students using plants to show uniqueness and care.

My mantra became "live like a plant," with the main tenet being that each species—indeed, each individual plant—has unique needs for optimal growth. We don't blame plants for failure to thrive if their needs aren't met, yet we are quick to denigrate our own need for rest (dormancy or shade), warmth and connection (sun), and even needing a specific nutrient (water, food, or supportive relationships). And over time, I started believing there is an important message here—one that can bring us back to a connection with nature and, thus, ourselves.

While we certainly share commonalities of humanness, no two people are exactly alike. Our needs and preferences were informed by our genes and our experiences. But in our increasingly loud and fast world, many of us have simply lost sight of what we once knew, instinctively, that we needed. Just as I was drawn to the woods as a kid, we all moved toward situations and conditions that would help us best grow, thrive, and find safety. But at some point, we started believing other people—even people we only knew by a profile picture or a social media account—when they told us what we *should* want or *should* do. And when that felt wrong, we tried doing it anyway! Can a cactus grow in a swamp just because we plant it there? You can have zero knowledge of horticulture and know that the answer is a resounding "no."

And so my wish is that this book will be a way back to *you*, with your Essential Nature as a guide. And through examples from the amazing, surprising, and non-apologetic world of plants, you will (re)learn how to honor what is unique about you and use that to inform what you need to truly thrive.

INTRODUCTION:

Essential Nature

*"We often forget that WE ARE NATURE.
Nature is not something separate from us. So
when we say that we have lost our connection to
nature, we've lost our connection to ourselves."*

— Andy Goldsworthy

*"Remember, all the answers are inside of you; you
only have to become quiet enough to hear them."*

— Debbie Ford

Plants don't need to "figure out who they are" or "find themselves." Neither, for that matter, do insects or animals. They are born knowing. They not only know how to survive but how to thrive.

Humans are no different. We just happen to have evolved to the point where we spend most of our time *thinking* instead of *knowing*. In fact, I would posit that we *did* know who we were—or at least what we wanted—when we were kids, before societal pressures and messages made us question ourselves. The answer to what we each need is still there inside of us, and it is not the same as what our parents, kids, partners, or best friends need. We are so bombarded with opinions, every day, nearly every minute, that we often have no idea where our needs end and our wants begin.

Recognizing that we, as humans, have unique and optimal growing conditions, the same as plants do, is at the heart of connecting to our Essential Nature. By accepting that we have limits to adapting within a fulfilling life, we are more easily able to reject the social codes and pressures that try to convince us to live in a way that is contrary to our true self. Just as a sunflower can't decide to become a rose (and would never attempt to), you are born to be the exact, amazing human that you are.

In learning to live like plants, we'll explore eight elements that impact a plant's ability to grow to its potential, as well as how it navigates environments that are less than optimal. We'll explore *climate zones, light and site, roots and nutrients, blooming, pollination, dormancy, disease resistance, and pests*. Although all eight elements impact every plant, the individual plant's response to those elements varies, even among those of the same species. We'll use the eight elements of plant survival to consider:

- belonging

- how we manage our energy

- how we find nourishment and sustenance

- what gifts we bring to the world

- how we impact future generations

- ways to find peace and rest

- how we each support our wellness and create healthy boundaries

Make no mistake—we *are* nature. We have inborn preferences and needs that make us unique. For example, I have a supersonic olfactory bulb—I can often smell someone's cologne before I see the whites of their eyes. Being near certain odors is distracting for me and can even become nauseating, so I naturally want to avoid strong odors. Even scents I love become unpleasant if they are too strong, like the sweet perfume of hyacinths or lilacs.

In other words, my Essential Nature detests strong scents. If I were a dog—the epitome of a sensitive sniffer—I would run away from smells I didn't like. But as a human, my brain has executive functioning capability. That means I can think, reason, and control my reactions in situations when I need to, though it *doesn't* mean that I can make myself like it.

Believe it or not, some plants react to touch in the same way dogs (or I) might react to odors. With just a whisper of a touch, the foliage of the sensitive plant (*Mimosa pudica*) instantly folds. The process is called *thigmonasty,* and it has to do with how chemicals function within the plant to shift water and nutrients when the stem of the plant is touched. Essentially, it collapses, likely in an effort to look less appetizing to pests that want to eat it.

Sensitive Plant (Mimosa pudica)

Mimosa pudica doesn't need to decide whether or not to react the way it does. It is this particular plant's natural, protective response to potential harm. This reaction is similar to a freeze response in the face of a physical assault. We've often heard the "fight or flight" response to a threat, but I have worked with many clients who have responded to a threat by freezing. Often in the aftermath of the threat, these clients feel guilt for not "doing something."

This is quite a poignant lesson. *Mimosa pudica* reacts naturally to protect itself. Humans are the same—we each have a natural response to threats. Often, this is simply the way we are wired. Sometimes our wiring is affected by the environment that shaped us. When we respond instinctively for self-protection, our brains may want to replay and question our actions after the fact. However, we could no more change our natural response to a threat than we could change our eye color or our foot size.

Jewelweed (*Impatiens capensis*), a native plant in the eastern United States, has seed pods that respond to touch by flying open with an explosion of seeds. This plant was a source of valuable medicinal properties for Native Americans, and with its enthusiastic sharing of seed, it has become one of the only native plants to out-compete invasive garlic mustard (*Alliaria petiolata*), which is an enormous threat to the woodlands of the eastern United States.

Imagine if jewelweed was able to control its seed dispersal. Would it try to temper itself lest other plants find it too forward or assertive? I think about the times I've kept ideas or thoughts to myself from a fear of being too loud or "too much" as a woman. Many times, those ideas were eventually broached by someone else and were welcomed.

As I matured professionally, I recognized that quiet observation was a superpower for me. Remember that "backward" girl of my childhood? After I was able to reframe my tendency for stillness within a group of people, I stopped feeling ashamed and was able to embrace it as a strength. That backward girl was always watching and processing, getting the lay of the land before contributing. Later, when I was told by a supervisor that I was too quiet in the first meeting I attended as an interim administrator, I replied that he might regret saying that after I learned the position a bit more. And lo and behold, when I eventually shared ideas in a way not too dissimilar from a jewelweed, he recognized that he had misjudged my quietness for weakness.

Recognizing whether your actions are an expression of your Essential Nature or an attempt to self-censure is key. Many female college students, usually in traditionally male-dominated majors like engineering or science, describe situations in which they were reluctant to speak in a class or lab environment because they were outnumbered by men. Women often hesitate to take up space in a way that men seem socialized to do from birth. Women might stay quiet or withhold their unique offerings because their brain stops them from expressing their true selves—their Essential Natures.

If jewelweed had a brain, would it question its Essential Nature? And if so, how tragic that its ability to heal and to help control a noxious plant that threatens its ecosystem may have never evolved! As silly as this comparison may seem, any time we try to tamp down or question our natural tendency, we deprive ourselves—and the world—of a gift. And from my experience, we often have an internal sense that offering that gift is right and okay, yet the programming of our brain often "thinks" us out of it.

Beyond these extreme cases of plant behavior, every plant—indeed, every organism—has a preferred environment. And the preferred environment varies from plant to plant, even those in the same species. The entire plant kingdom includes 300,000 species of plants! We would never assume every plant prefers the same environment, yet we frequently pressure ourselves and others to conform to an "acceptable" human standard.

Even a single family of plants includes thousands of species. For example, the sunflower family (*Asteraceae*) includes about 24,000 species. The amazing variety of sunflowers is a source of delight, even to plant laypersons. Yet we are often fearful of diversity in other humans and shameful of non-conformity in ourselves.

The *hardiness zone*—the geographical region defined by the range of yearly temperatures—and the continuum of sunlight needed by individual plant species are two aspects of determining the preferred environment for a plant. Most importantly, plants need to be able to survive the lowest temperatures of the region where they are growing. Additionally, the leaves of plants that thrive in shade can burn to a crisp in the sun, and the plants themselves could literally die. Conversely, plants that need full sun will fail to thrive and flower if they are planted in the shade. Those plants didn't *choose* to need those conditions to grow optimally. And unlike humans, they don't have a brain with a frontal lobe, so they can't just decide to make the best of it. However, their Essential Nature is to *try* to find a more optimal situation without questioning if they *should*. Or, more importantly, if other plants think they should.

Just as humans need sleep to survive, plants—even shade plants—need light. Therefore, all plants will naturally grow toward light, even if it's a candle flame in a dark room. They don't *decide* to do that so much as it's simply part of their nature. They don't question it ("So will my companion plants feel I'm rejecting them if I grow in the opposite direction?"). They don't have the worries we might, courtesy of the limbic system in our human brain, to question their own needs. Or to worry how their needs will make others feel.

And plants that are in a less than optimal environment don't compare themselves to their companion plants that are thriving. They simply continue to try to adjust to their own situations and grow the best they can.

Sometimes plants can get too much of a good thing. One of the most common reasons houseplants die is because we water them too often! But for some plants, ample water won't kill them—they need it. We plant nerds talk about certain plants liking "wet feet." This means that they need more water than might be typical for the average plant. Other plants, like, say, a cactus, *don't* want wet feet. They will get spongy and mushy and will likely die—they need *less* water than what might be typical. There is not a single, correct amount of water for every plant.

When plants are in an environment that has unsuitable moisture conditions for their Essential Nature, they will extend their roots toward what they need. They will intuitively grow and proliferate in the direction that is most advantageous. If they like wet feet and they can spread toward the part of the landscape with poor drainage, they will! They don't wonder if something is wrong with them for needing more or less water than other plants. Their Essential Nature needs what it needs.

Plants don't look at other plants on social media and ruminate on why those other plants look so happy in the desert while they, themselves, feel like their leaves are burning to a crisp after a few hours of direct sun. And plants that grow best situated a distance from other plants don't feel guilty or stupid because the lily of the valley across the yard are packed together like thriving extroverts. They just grow as they need to grow. They don't compare themselves to others or beat themselves up or decide that the lily of the valley must be the ones growing in the *correct* way.

I have done two things for a very long time—tend plants and counsel humans. I know figuring out what we truly want in our lives is possible, and we can look to nature for guidance in finding it.

You might be thinking, "Wait, plants are great and all, but I don't really *care* about them. So I don't think I *want* to live like a plant." Well, in a sense, we already *do* live like plants. We try to find the best life conditions to help us create a life we want. However, it's our thinking brain and our social scripts that can end up causing us to try creating the life we're *told* to want. That makes us similar to plants that aren't growing where or how they need to in order to truly thrive. And instead of looking at our environment to figure out what needs to change, we often assume there's something wrong with *us* when we can't grow to our full potential.

Maybe you're a tomato plant that gets dozens of little blossoms, but you can't ever successfully convert them to tomatoes. Or maybe you're a sunflower, and you have tall bushy, leafy stems but your flowers are puny and, to be honest, not really … sunny. Or you're growing with a group of orange flowers but you're not orange, and you don't like standing out in the crowd. Or you *want* to stand out, but you're crowded and overlooked because, well, orange is so damn bright!

When I have plants or clients that aren't thriving, I assess their growing environments. With clients, I help them consider what they have learned from past environments and how their Essential Natures inform what will help them become fulfilled and content. Notice I said my plants *or* my clients—it's a framework, and it can work for nearly any living thing. You don't have to be a tree hugger or have a green thumb or even grow a houseplant to use the guidelines of plant health to help focus on what you need to live stronger, healthier, and more vibrantly. All living things need some of the same things: a hospitable environment, a solid foundation, nutrients, ideal growing conditions, and recognition of our relationship to others.

We're going to assess our own environment through the framework of the eight elements of a plant's ecosystem or community. Each of these elements relates to a task of fulfillment in our lives. These range from deciding if we're in the right zone to find belonging to considering how the nuanced sun-and-shade continuum of everyday life recharges our energy through connection and solitude. We'll explore how the gifts we share with the world reflect the analogy of blooming in the plant world, and we'll connect with the "pollinators" of life that help generate and sustain those gifts. We'll ponder how plants' unapologetic need for dormancy can empower us to recognize our unique need for rest and renewal. And finally, we'll consider how plants protect themselves from pests and disease as a way to inform our own need to establish boundaries and prioritize wellness. Let's start by discovering how plants know where they belong—their optimal climate zone—and determine if we're in our human zone for belonging.

CHAPTER 1 CLIMATE ZONES:

Where do you find belonging?

"Grow where you are planted."

— Unknown

*"Growth is painful. Change is painful. But, nothing is
as painful as staying stuck where you do not belong."*

— N. R. Narayana Murthy

All plants have an optimal temperature range at which they grow best. These
ranges are divided into geographical areas called climate zones, and they are
based on the coldest annual temperature of that region. Plants are assigned
to zones based on their *hardiness*—the lowest temperature in which they
can survive. In the United States, zones 9–11 are considered tropical. (The
higher the zone number, the warmer the average winter temperature is.)

Plants from tropical zones cannot survive winter temperatures in my
zone 7 garden because it simply gets too cold. Of course, the summer
temperatures are important, too, but because freezing temperatures tend to
be the determinant of plant survival, we focus on the plant's cold hardiness in
establishing zones. There are some plants that we would call cold hardy in my
zone that struggle in the heat of our summers, but this is often tempered by

where we site it—or place it—in the landscape. Thus, being able to survive winters in Pennsylvania doesn't make for a "better" plant, nor does thriving in the heat of an Arizona summer. Part of each plant's Essential Nature is the zone where it belongs.

However, when we make choices about what plants to choose for our own gardens, we need to consider something deeper than simply the number of the zone. Often, plants co-evolve with the pollinators they need to support their reproduction, as well as with the other plants that support them—or won't outcompete them. The level of humidity and the nutrients in the soil are also important to consider. Often, a lack of thriving can result from conditions that may not be obvious at first.

Starting with the correct climate for plant health is non-negotiable. If you choose a plant that can't survive winter, then all the pollinators or soil nutrients or perfect rainfall amounts are for naught. When considering zone, we need to prioritize the cold limit but also consider the ecosystem.

We need to do the same for ourselves: Knowing our Thrivability Zone—the human equivalent of hardiness zone for plants—is paramount, but recognizing the microclimate and surrounding ecosystem is also important if we truly want to flourish. Let's explore human Thrivability Zones and how to know where we truly belong.

What does *belonging* mean for humans? I'm willing to bet that you had a certain feeling inside when you read the word *belonging*. We might first think of experiences we've had where we knew, deep in our hearts, we didn't belong. I had that feeling in one of my jobs. I felt like an outsider the minute I stepped into my office, and I was uncomfortable for the entire year and a half that I worked there. I felt supported by my boss, and I knew I was making a positive impact on many students, but I felt like I was a palm tree trying to grow in Iceland. While I could make human adjustments, I didn't feel like I belonged in that environment. I was outside my human Thrivability Zone.

Feeling that we belong includes how we experience the actions of others, as well as how we instinctively respond to the environment around us. Feeling accepted and included is vital, but so is having an inner sense of "rightness." In my job situation, I instinctively knew I was trying to live, professionally, in an environment where I could not grow and fully express my Essential Nature.

I was the sole counselor in my building after working for years as part of a larger counseling staff, where there was always someone right next door or down the hall to turn to for advice or a laugh. And for the first time, I was working with young children, not teens, so my duties were vastly different, as was the way I could engage and create change. I managed—and even had some wonderful victories—but I wasn't getting the type of warmth and connection that fostered my sense of belonging as part of a team.

There were also some clinicians in other buildings who created a cold (winter) environment for which I wasn't prepared. Remember in the plant world, winter is a make-or-break situation for survival. For humans, feeling frozen out of work relationships or projects will severely limit thriving. Perhaps I could have had a more robust hardiness, but this lack of true connection, to me, felt like a winter that was way too cold and long! Again, I was used to a connected and mutually supportive team, but feeling that I was a transplant that wasn't fully welcome as part of the ecosystem contributed to my feeling a lack of belonging.

Sometimes humans feel a lack of belonging in the very environment into which they were born. I used to work with high schoolers, and many of them would tell me that they couldn't wait to graduate so they could move away or find a college in a different state. But guess what happened with many of them? While they loved the initial excitement of a new location, and maybe they even bloomed and flourished, after a while, they missed home. Their burst of growth just leveled off and they didn't feel they were in the right place anymore. In a sense, they grew and reached a point where their first zone now felt right for them. They knew how to get what they needed where they were raised; they belonged there.

For others, they may never have felt like home was … well, home. Unlike plants that sprout from a seed, humans can "germinate" in an environment that isn't hospitable to their growth. For them, moving away isn't for the excitement or to get away from mom and dad or their boring ol' hometown. They know, somehow, that they will thrive somewhere else. And when they do migrate to an environment that feels aligned with their needs, and they put down roots there, they often prosper—even when others said they wouldn't. These are young people that recognize and connect to their Essential Nature. Even in a world where they may have received messages about what career they *should* have or where they *should* go to college or how they *should* live, they listened to their own inner knowing.

Having worked in public schools in a relatively conservative political and religious area, my teenage students sometimes felt stifled by the values of their parents or their larger community. One of the most serious issues I encountered was a young female who came out as gay to her parents in her first year of high school. I watched her struggle to deny her Essential Nature, as her parents were harshly vocal about their disapproval. Ultimately, she was overwhelmed by the lack of warmth and acceptance and attempted to take her own life. She survived, but it took many years before she was able to find a new environment where she could finally experience belonging.

In the same way we can't expect a sunflower to produce roses, we essentially have parts of our being that are expressions of our true nature. Although the issues of sexual orientation and gender identity have created emotional and sometimes violent confrontations in certain societies, communities, and religions, a human's way of being and their needs that support thriving are as unique to them as the specific method of pollination or sexual fluidity of certain plants.

Many holly species (genus *Ilex*) are *dioecious*, meaning that individual plants are either male and female. There needs to be at least one male plant growing in the vicinity of the female in order for fertilization to commence and eventually produce berries. However, some holly species are *monoecious* and have both male and female parts on the same plant. Tomato plants (*Solanum lycopersicum*) have both male and female parts on each individual blossom, and papaya (*Carica papaya*) blooms can be male, female, or hermaphroditic. If conditions exist that threaten pollination, papaya flowers can change their sex to ensure reproduction.

In nature, we are often awestruck by these types of adaptability in plant reproduction, but we don't extend that same appreciation of sexual diversity to our fellow humans. If nature allows—even amplifies—fluidity in plants, surely we can recognize that the same continuum of rich variability exists for all species of organisms. And if you, as a plant, might be one of the amazingly fluid species yourself, know that nature makes it clear this is not an aberration but rather an aspect of nature that brings a delightful continuum of gifts to the world.

So what determines your Thrivability Zone, and how do you know if you're planted in the right one?

The answer is inside you, but sometimes it's so deep, it's hard to sense it at first. Consider some of these questions: Do you feel that you belong where you are right now? In your home? In your neighborhood? Do you fit into your work environment and feel like a valued and respected member of the team? Are you accepted for exactly who you are and what strengths you bring to the table? Do you feel like your partner and your family supports your Essential Nature, and do you feel comfortable expressing it?

As humans, part of finding our Thrivability Zone is being aware of what—and who—is growing around us. Like my experience working solo without the support of others of my species (fellow counselors), I could certainly continue to survive, but the other features of the environment, including the different plants growing around me, left me feeling alienated and unfulfilled.

So in addition to being curious about areas where you instinctively feel a lack of belonging, getting clear about your specific needs and wholeheartedly accepting yourself is the undeniable first step. Each subsequent chapter will examine more specific facets of how to recognize and support your Essential Nature, but let's start with thinking a bit more about you, your unique attributes, and how they mesh (or don't) with your current environment.

Humans, like many plants, have some zonal variability. Nature overall is meant to be adaptable. Very few plants can survive in only one climate zone. For example, raspberries (*Rubus idaeus)* are hardy in zones 3–9, while common blackberries (*Rubus allegheniensis)* are limited to zones 5–9. This means that raspberries can withstand winter temperatures that are 10 degrees colder than blackberries. For humans, this may not seem like a huge deal. And truly, it may not be dire if our human Thrivability Zone changes a bit. But some people are more sensitive to change than others. Some of us have a more narrow band of zones where we can thrive. Or we might already be right at the edge of our ideal zone. Because we're humans with an evolved frontal lobe, most of us can use strategies to adjust to less-than-optimal environments. Our strength is in our resilience. Recognizing the aspects of your current zone and figuring out how to adapt to succeed is the goal.

Let's think like a plant. If you were to discover yourself for sale in the garden center, you would have a plant tag—a little plastic label often stuck into the soil of your pot—that covers your attributes. In the case of plants, it usually includes common name, scientific (Latin) name, mature size and habit, sun and water requirements, bloom time, and hardiness zone. It also commonly has a picture of what the plant will look like if all those growing conditions are met—the flowers and sometimes the leaves, if the foliage is the main physical attribute.

As we dive more into human Thrivability Zones, imagine what this might look like for you. What would you look like if you were thriving right now? I would venture to guess that, as a kid, you could probably fill out your plant tag instinctively. However, as adults, most of us have misplaced the plant tag of our youth.

It might be helpful to start with some familiar examples, so let's explore some of the more common plants we might find in a garden center. Regardless of where you live, there will be plants in your local garden center that would not survive if planted outside; they are not able to withstand some aspect of your climate. These would either be grown as annuals or houseplants. This is a totally valid existence, as the gardener would ensure that the plants in their care get what they need to grow and thrive; in our case, we need to evaluate whether we are getting our own needs met. This begins with considering our own Essential Nature and whether our current zone is truly where we belong. Does it match the Thrivability Zone that's on our internal plant tag?

Let's say you're a philodendron, an easy to grow tropical plant that can tolerate many different growing conditions as long as temperatures don't get too cold. And maybe you pretty much develop and stretch in nearly any situation, as long as you have enough light and room. You are pretty lowkey, but you like to move into new areas. Philodendrons are quite adaptable and don't suffer too much if they need to be confined in a pot.

However, sometimes philodendrons are *too* easy. Because they can continue to survive a wide range of conditions, they may appear healthy to the untrained eye. But take a look at their roots and you may find that they have been continuing to grow even as they are *rootbound*. This means that their roots are too big for the pot, so they grow around and around the bottom, limiting their ability to spread and obtain moisture and nutrients.

If you are growing somewhere where you are trying to keep up appearances, or where the environment around you isn't supporting your need for nutrients or establishing healthy roots, it may be time to consider whether another zone (or, in the case of the philodendron, a larger pot) would allow you to thrive.

Or, maybe you're more like an orchid! Orchids are fussy—some might say high maintenance. The term "high maintenance" when applied to people isn't always flattering. So let's say, instead, that you're "exotic." And actually, as we'll learn later, while orchids may appear fussy and delicate, they have cornered the market when it comes to protective adaptations. They utilize their uniqueness and beauty as amazing boundaries against pests. And if you see them in their native environment, typically a rainforest, they will take your breath away.

Orchids are a tremendous example of plants that appear to be vulnerable, but they simply know what they need to live in all their glory. And they leverage those strengths to fight for survival in areas where human encroachment threatens them with extinction. To the outside observer, they may be judged as too needy, but they continue to do what they do, no explanations and no apologies. And if anything, it is what will save them.

Do you like a lot of deep connections with your community, family, or friends? You could be a cactus! In situations that might burn others to a crisp, you thrive. That might mean you like high stimulation to be productive. Or it might mean, simply, that you like your environment (home, friendships, workplace) to feel warm and consistent with a lot of communication and closeness. You might mistake this need for deep connection with not needing down time—you just want to bask in the warmth of your people all the time. But make no mistake: cacti definitely have downtime. Often, nights in the desert are cold! They are just fine in that cold darkness. And would you believe that there is a cactus native to my state of Pennsylvania? That goes to show you that they are a more varied family of plants than we might assume. If a cactus is in the best zone, it's a true thriver.

But as you can imagine, cacti prefer dry soil. So what happens to cacti when the rare storm occurs? Well, they kinda shut down. It's not uncommon for people that want to live with the consistent warmth of connection to feel overwhelmed or hopeless when they suffer through a loss or the end of a relationship. But do you know what happens to cacti after they recover from the deluge of rain? They bloom. Spectacularly.

Now you may be thinking about those spines—not very warm and welcoming, huh? Well, those spines have quite a useful purpose. They are often what help a cactus gather moisture in an arid environment. Yes, those same spines can be a barrier, but perhaps we can think of them as a boundary; those organisms that understand and respect the cactus know how to navigate them and avoid harm.

We will explore all of these aspects more closely—boundaries, roots, nutrients, and more—in upcoming chapters. For now, start to consider the varied needs of these plant examples—the diversity and amazingness of the plant kingdom is nearly boundless. The same is true for humans—for *you!*

So what makes the cold the main defining characteristic of hardiness zones? Winter—cold conditions—are often the key time for plants to rest and recharge for the next growing season. In more temperate or even arid areas, it can be the rainy season, as I mentioned in the case of the cactus, that triggers plants to take a rest and prepare for new growth or blooming.

And while all organisms need a way to recharge, we don't often consider this for ourselves. We tend to set the unattainable expectation for ourselves (or others) that we need to be "on" all the time. But nature knows: rest is non-negotiable, and there is no wrong way to practice self-care and build your energy.

Dormancy is essential for healthy, optimal growth; we can think of this as the loose equivalent to sleep for plants. Often, perennials (plants that return each year) die back and look like they're goners. Like deciduous trees that shed their leaves and embrace the skeletal look until spring, perennials in a winter landscape are often dried and brown. Cold is also important to seeds, as they need chilly temperatures to eventually crack their shells so that they can germinate. Some seeds can actually wait through several winters until they have optimal conditions to germinate. This is what they do instinctively to carry on their species. Pretty amazing to live through several winters just waiting to show their stuff, right? Makes the term "late bloomer" kind of high praise.

Remember the example of my young students who knew their birth climates weren't the healthiest for them? Sometimes it's harder to figure out what is causing your failure to thrive in your current zone. It might take experiencing another zone for you to find what's missing on your plant tag.

Take the herb dill (*Anethum graveolens*), for example. Dill isn't hardy in my current climate zone. So one spring a couple years ago, I was surprised to find my dill survived the winter. It was a milder winter than usual, and it was planted in a sheltered spot. But even though it survived, it certainly didn't thrive that second year. And by the third spring, it was gone. It couldn't continue to find the reserves to recover.

We, as humans, sometimes find ourselves in similar situations. We often adapt to less-than-favorable situations to survive our early environment, only to recognize as young adults (or older adults) that our adaptations, while allowing us to survive, actually limit our ability to flourish.

Conversely, a new environment can initially affect our growth if it feels too different. When I worked at a university, international students often talked to me about their difficulty adjusting to the quietness of the campus. Many of them lived in urban areas in their home country, and they sometimes talked of insomnia brought about by the heavy silence of the farm fields and sleepy town surrounding the campus—they missed the constant noise!

As a country girl, living in a noisy city would make me feel like a water lily trying to grow on a rocky mountainside, but the diversity of zone preferences is what makes nature, including human nature, not only fascinating, but viable! Imagine if we were all cacti or sunflowers or water lilies or palm trees. What a boring, monochromatic world that would be.

When are plants vulnerable to succumbing to the wrong hardiness zone? It's often when humans get involved, and we try to grow them where they don't (or can't) belong. For example, we might be lured in by the amazing array of healthy flowering plants in the local garden center and make the mistake of thinking all of these plants can live outside all year. In the same way, we can make the mistake of thinking that what works for another person—your best friend, the influencer on TikTok, your partner—will work for you.

As we emerged back into the world, stunned and squinting against the light, after the worst of COVID, the work-from-home culture was cemented into the corporate world. Although in my work for a university, being back in person was crucial, I was surprised to find that many of my therapist colleagues in the private practice world wanted to go fully remote—teletherapy only. Many potential clients went along with it—after all, it certainly made things easier: No driving to an office, just prop yourself up and turn on your camera.

However, the amount of non-verbal data therapists lose when connecting with clients over a computer screen is astronomical. (Spoiler: I'm a bit biased on this topic.) What does the client's energy feel like? Are they wearing clean clothes? How did their body look walking into the office? How is their eye contact? For a long time, this part of communication, which by varying estimates can be up to 90 percent of the tone of our message, seemed to be easily left behind. But slowly, I have seen both clinicians and clients start leaning back toward in-person sessions. While remote therapy does work for some, others find that too cold.

And lest you think cold always equates to less thriving, it's actually quite impossible to grow many plants in the heat of the southern United States! Remember that many plants need cold temperatures to go dormant, rest, and build their energy reserves. In fact, when plants cannot get the low temperatures they need to trigger dormancy, it's a game changer—not only for the species affected, but for the ecosystem surrounding it.

Plants evolve to coexist with other plants and, more importantly, with specific pollinators. In our modern world, there are two major issues that impact these ecological relationships: human interference—clearing land for homes, commerce, or farming—and climate change (which is a secondary consequence of human interference).

A catastrophic example: The plant that supports monarch butterfly caterpillars is milkweed (*Asclepias)*. It is crucial that monarchs have access to this plant all along their route to and from Mexico as they continue to spawn on their migration route each year. In my native Pennsylvania, as well as surrounding states, stands of milkweed are disappearing due to clear-cutting and land development. This makes it increasingly difficult for monarchs to find the plant colonies they need to lay their eggs, threatening the very existence of these amazing butterflies.

Overall, the loss of wild and native flowering plants due to land development threatens many species of bees, butterflies, moths, and even birds that rely on wild berries. Even in areas that are not clearcut, pesticide and herbicide use has deleterious results, as well.

In the case of climate change, warmer weather and altered rainfall patterns can disrupt the delicate timing between when flowers bloom and when their specific pollinators most need access to the pollen. For example, the Mojave poppy bee evolved to pollinate only a specific species of poppy (*Papaver),* and the bee needs the pollen to feed its young at a specific point in their breeding. The timing of flowering is changing due to warming temperatures, meaning that there is an increasing mismatch in the timing of blooms related to the activity of the bees. The worst case scenario is that the bees are unable to support their young and they die off.

What is the takeaway? Humans trying to succeed in the wrong zone obviously impacts their whole being—mind, body, and spirit. And sometimes, events or situations that may seem insignificant have ripple effects. And we don't often think of the impact on our entire community—our ecosystem. Ironically, we often believe that we need to just try harder in situations where we feel depressed, depleted, or downtrodden.

Yet when a plant is struggling, we look at its soil, its nutrients and water, its light source. We never blame a plant for compromised growth. Yet, every single day, we blame ourselves for struggling in environments that deplete our body, our spirit, and our self-worth. That lack of thriving—as well as attributing it to our own failure—affects our partners, our children, our work, and our colleagues, as well as our wider community. But more than that, it affects our ability to overcome challenges because we assume we are the problem instead of considering the soil and the air around us.

Because of environmental climate change, the hardiness zone where I live has changed twice in the few decades I've been gardening. This means, roughly, that winter temperatures are now 10 degrees warmer on average than they were in 1990. Furthermore, weather patterns are more unstable and rainfall predictions seem more erratic. Although this may not seem like a huge deal for people, it certainly is for plants—and by extension, other organisms that evolved to rely on those plants! Dormancy means that temperatures need to be consistently cold, so having the thermometer dip and rise too often literally confuses the plant. If it breaks dormancy too soon, the resulting new foliage may be killed by frost burn when the temperature drops again.

Spring bulbs, like daffodils and tulips, need a certain number of days at temperatures as low as 32°F (freezing) to go dormant and conserve energy so that they are ready to bloom in spring. This process is called *vernalization*.

While dormancy refers to a suspension of growth—a rest—in response to cold (or other environmental changes, like an increase or decrease in rainfall), vernalization is the process of cold temperatures being a catalyst for inducing a plant's ability to flower.

As temperatures in my geographical area become warmer in winter due to climate change, these bulbs are blooming earlier in the spring. This could eventually impact their viability, as they won't get enough days at lower temperatures to sufficiently vernalize. And a surprise frost could burn the leaves that raised their heads above ground too soon. But the plants don't know that. They just instinctively respond to warmer temperatures, having no idea the last potential frost date, based on a human calendar, is still weeks away.

Paying attention to how we function in our zone is key to managing our dormancy or vernalization. And accompanying that is how the climate of life around us supports our unique need for the human equivalent of these processes and whether we sense that we belong there—that our needs are being met.

Now that you have this context, think about how you function in your current zone. You just might discover that you're planted in a zone that isn't congruent with your hardiness. Remember, *hardiness*, like thrivability, isn't a continuum of positive to negative. A plant that can't survive winters in zone 7 isn't a bad plant or a lazy plant. It's just a plant that belongs in a specific zone that will encourage its growth or more dramatically, not cause its death. A tulip that only blooms for one week of the year, then needs to rest and build energy for next year, isn't "underutilizing its potential." It's just doing what it needs to do to be the best and most radiant tulip it can be. A seed that sits in the cold, dark soil for years isn't loafing around and wasting its life; it's waiting until the conditions are right to have its *best* life. As humans, we need what we need, just like plants do!

So let's ponder a few things. Many specific populations of people struggle more to find a zone of belonging than others might. For example, having a condition brought on by chronic inflammation, hormonal disorders, or other special needs requires a unique dormancy cycle for wellness. Often those who suffer with autoimmune issues aren't adequately understood and supported by family, friends, and especially supervisors in work environments. Too often, employers want workers who need little or no dormancy to keep producing; this is untenable, for any organism. In fact, not honoring the unique needs of these people often makes them sicker, just like a plant that we try to grow where it is too cold or too hot—its survival is in jeopardy.

Likewise for populations of color or those with gender identities or sexual preferences that don't fall into the mainstream or socially accepted binary "choices," as mentioned previously: There may be zones in which certain people could never thrive, as much as they might want to adapt to the climate or are pressured by people they love to do so.

Sometimes for humans, dormancy may literally be about the seasons, just like it is for plants. Some of us feel sad with less sunlight in the winter months. This may be part of our dormancy process. Or maybe some people prepare to produce in the coming season, like teachers or actors preparing for a movie role or contractors strategizing for a new project. These situations may be more like vernalization: the downtime is in anticipation of blooming!

Conversely, humans' mental and physical health may seem to follow a seasonal cycle. Seasonal affective disorder, for example, is characterized by a depressed mood often occurring in fall or winter months, and sometimes includes impacts to sleep, appetite, and energy levels. As a therapist who tries to consider the bigger view of a client's ecosystem, I sometimes wonder if their distress is increased by believing they *shouldn't* feel sad or want to hibernate. Imagine if daffodil bulbs believed that resting for most of the year made them lazy or meant that they were sick? We would be deprived of the amazing sweeps of color when they "wake" from all that rest to bring us explosions of blooms.

Feeling depressed or anxious or generally unwell might simply mean that we need to think about the entire climate of our life. Let me be clear,

I am not minimizing those with true, diagnosable mental health concerns. However, there are often situations that exist as part of one's zone that contribute to the feeling that one doesn't belong in their current life. I would suggest reflecting on your needs in the context of dormancy or vernalization, and see if it yields any inspiration for increasing wellness by honoring your Essential Nature. Are you responding to messages from social media, family, or supervisors that you need to be producing and blooming all the time with no rest? Do you hesitate establishing boundaries around the need for self-care because you don't want others to think you're weak or can't pull your weight? Eventually, your body will take the break you need, whether you want it to or not. Remember, our Essential Nature requires that we find ways to use dormancy to build our strength and live our best life. It also helps inform us about climates that don't foster a sense of belonging.

By now, you might be getting the sense that your current life zone isn't supporting your sense of belonging. You're not aligned with your Essential Nature, and the climate is not giving you the peak environment in which to blossom. If you always feel pushed to produce or put the needs of others before your own or live/be/act in an "acceptable" manner, maybe you're living in a zone that's too hot—you don't have the vernalization time you need. Winter is too short and warm. Or what if you feel the coldness of being unsupported and not getting an opportunity to grow? Your zone has a winter that is too cold and a growing season that is too brief.

It is possible that you cannot find true fulfillment without either living in your optimal zone or finding healthy ways to adjust to the zone where you find yourself. And that's the biggest question: Could you continue to survive where you are? Sure, maybe you could function like the tropical plants we bring inside for winter. They will survive, but they—and you—may not realize their full potential. But still, you're probably wondering if maybe you'll be happy adjusting. Certainly there are plants that do just fine adapting, right? Yes, some do. And here's where we, as ambulating, frontal-lobe-possessing humans, might have an advantage. The question you need to answer is, do you stay put and try to adapt? Or do you move on?

Let's consider dandelions (*Taraxacum officinale*), for instance. They will grow in zone 2–11. They won't necessarily thrive in every environment, but they will live. Native to Europe and Asia, dandelions have naturalized to most areas of the United States. They are resilient and can even be found growing in cracks in the sidewalk. Although many people find them an annoying weed, I would contend that this is because they simply don't conform to what we want them to be! They are truly underappreciated—a marginalized population of plants. Indeed, all parts of the dandelion plant—leaves, roots and flowers—are edible and rich in several nutrients. Both plants and seeds are even sold for those who want to grow them intentionally for culinary or medicinal uses. This is where they would find belonging, if they had a brain with a frontal lobe.

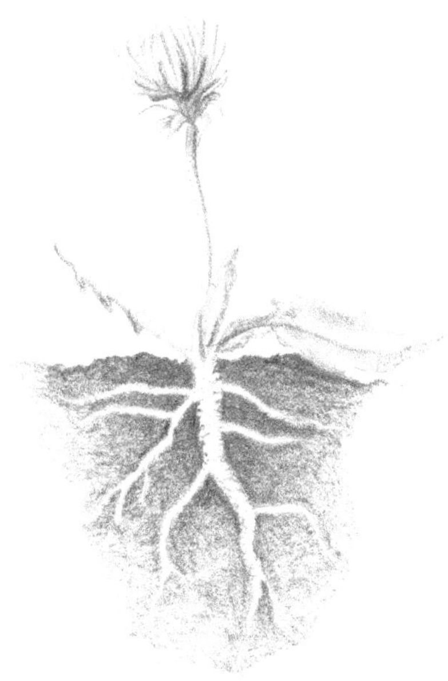

Dandelion (Taraxacum officinale)

There are many plants that are tough and able to generalize to several zones. Although these types of plants are often considered weeds by many, there are others who admire their tenacity and their value. I can tell you from my experience, even dandelions don't flourish everywhere in their hardiness zones. They might not flower, for instance. But they are living and contributing something to the world. Point being, it doesn't matter how others view dandelions. Remember there are no bad plants. And dandelions can no more change their Essential Natures or their hardiness zones than they could decide to bloom bright red. But they are amazingly adaptable.

So it's no secret that in life, as in nature, zones never *really* remain unchanged. Life events change our climate—things like relationship endings, job transitions, or loss and grief. They also impact how hot and stressful life feels: a new school year, needing to learn new tasks at work, a partner's illness, or a child's emergency. When levels of stress run high, or we experience inertia from depression, grief, or other isolating events, it can truly feel like a climate change; our whole world—or way of being—has shifted.

So how does it look when a human adapts to a zone that isn't the best one for thriving?

Well, this type of human adaptation often relies on two aspects: boundaries and communication. We will explore these concepts more in chapter 8, but for now, simply put: Recognizing your Essential Nature, as well as the zone that is optimal for you, will inform how you adapt. If you are not taking the steps you need to get the rest and dormancy you need to be healthy and content, it will require setting limits on your efforts in order to protect your energy. You will then need to communicate what you need in ways that will make your boundaries clear, and start to enact change in areas where you don't feel that "rightness" of belonging or alignment with your zone.

Perhaps you have been slowly adapting, but didn't recognize it. What if you used to thrive just fine in your zone but at some point you started to struggle? It's likely that the zone around you changed and now you're at the limit of your cold hardiness. It's as if you're a dandelion that started life in zone 4 but now you find yourself in zone 2, the coldest zone you can tolerate. You're still living, but maybe you no longer grow as large or have as many flowers as you've had in past years. What if you have no more "adapting" in you? What do plants do when they can no longer adapt to the changing climate? Obviously they can't use rational thought to figure it out. They just do what they need to, if they can. And what do they do if the change is drastic enough, which our current state of climate change certainly is? Believe it or not, they move.

Yes, plants move. Well actually, it would be a bit inaccurate to say *individual* plants move. It's more like they move *as a species*. The mechanism by which that happens is typically seed dispersal. And we are talking about *big* movement—potentially 60 miles in a century. Think about navigating that distance through no other means than reliance on pollinators, like birds and other animals, as well as the wind. The members of your ecosystem literally save your family! See how important the environment around us is?

As the Earth has warmed, areas that were previously covered with ice have thawed, and species like pines moved into those areas when the microclimate where they had previously thrived became too warm for them to live. Likewise, some plants have expanded their geographical range into areas that were previously too cold for their survival, as it warmed enough for their seeds to germinate and thrive there.

When plants reach a point at which they can't continue to grow in their previous geographical area, they instinctively head for environments where they *can* grow. And while they certainly can't ambulate like we can, they may have an advantage in that they can't question their choice to just go. They don't need to worry they might be making a mistake or they won't like their new neighbors or their new coworkers. They know, inside, "Hey, this ain't working," and they make the move.

Maybe you can relate. Perhaps there have been situations that caused you to recognize that the world around you was no longer hospitable to your optimal growth. Maybe it was fine—or even *more* than fine—for a while, but slowly it just wasn't anymore. And you reached a point where you realized that your Essential Nature wasn't happy. You were surviving, but you weren't thriving. Yet you hesitated.

It is a common human condition to feel or sense something is wrong, but then our brain steps in and elbows the *amygdala* to fire up our fear response. The amygdala is part of the emotional processing system in our brain—our *limbic system*—and she does her job *very* well. She learns what has harmed us in the past, and if she even perceives a hint of it in any situation or experience, she can overreact like a smoke detector howls over a piece of burning toast. This creates fear.

The frontal lobe translates fear as, "I can't/shouldn't make a change!" That pesky frontal lobe processing can give you every possible reason to stay where you are, in spite of your inner self recognizing that Things. Are. Not. Okay. Plus, you're deep into it—you've connected to parts of your current zone that make it harder to just pull up stakes and move on.

So how do you know when you've reached your maximum adaptation? Consider the aspects that have rendered the current climate inhospitable. What events or situations contributed to climate change in your life? Are there relationships that no longer support your growth? Or that might even be harmful? Do you feel disenfranchised by your work? Have all the world political changes or the 24-hour news cycle or social media static made you feel twitchy, depressed, anxious? Even those global issues are part of human climate change.

What if it wasn't gradual? What if you have a huge, sudden change in the climate around you? Remember, as humans, we all eventually have periodic harsh winters—times when we experience a loss—such as when a pet dies, or we graduate and friendships shift, or we suffer with a temporary illness. Within our individual zones, we can "go dormant" and survive to flower again. We can be like the cactus after the rainy season overwhelms us and eventually explode with flowers when we find our footing again. Or we can quietly conserve energy and maximize it for the coming spring. We can adapt, especially if the zone that changed only affected one major area of life. But what if it's even bigger than that? What if a change in one area of life changes your *whole* life?

Imagine that you need to *vernalize* (embrace the cold as a prelude to flowering again) to recover from a divorce, or a job loss, or any life change that requires reassessment and huge transformation. You recognize that this is a much different winter than you've navigated before. It's colder and it's longer. The zone *around* you has definitely changed as you've lost relationships or situations that supported your renewal. Your life is the epitome of climate change. Maybe you believe that you can withstand this winter, if you have enough time to build your reserves. But as the seasons go, spring is still coming. Life is still happening, and you can't vernalize—or even rest in dormancy—forever. You need a longer pause but the stressors are pushing and pushing at you. Or you feel like you're one of those seeds, waiting in the cool, dark soil for the right time to germinate into the next "you." Being able to adapt to a changing climate is certainly a strength and a boon to survival. But so is the ability to recognize the severity of the change … and move on.

I know firsthand the combination of grief and acceptance that goes along with recognizing that my Thrivability Zone, where I felt connected and had a true sense of contentment, no longer supported my healthy growth. Indeed, it was slowly killing me. It has happened to me more than once in my career. But the last one was a doozy.

As a therapist, working with other therapists can definitely create an environment that is uniquely supportive. Until it's not. I think we like to think that people in certain professions share positive traits: Engineers are always rational and ordered, nurses and doctors always make healthy life choices, mental health counselors are fully self-aware and supportive of others. In reality, some of the most dysfunctional professionals I've known have had advanced degrees in mental health.

This is not always a huge deal; we all have our issues, right? But there are two times when it *is* a concern. The first is when the dysfunction affects clients. Fortunately, this is quite rare, at least from my experience. The other is when the dysfunction takes the form of cruelty and toxicity—*and* that person is your new boss. This was one situation where I realized that the climate zone where I existed professionally had changed. The warmth and client-focused environment became unpredictable and toxic. It was too cold for true rest and energizing; I would've had to go dormant for months to survive, but that much winter and that deep cold isn't my zone at all. Plus, it was too hot to grow without struggling just to have enough professional sustenance. The distance from one end of the work environment spectrum to the other easily doubled. Way colder connections and, when the heat was on, it was Death Valley temperatures. I felt like I was a pansy flower—lover of cool temperatures—happily growing and blooming, that suddenly found itself in the middle of the Sahara—in July.

Although that may sound like a dramatic comparison, it is exactly how I felt—like I was struggling just to survive, and I kept getting more ragged and crisp. And I certainly couldn't bloom! Not being able to survive in this new climate zone didn't mean there was something lacking in me, just as there is nothing wrong with plants that can't grow where they aren't meant to grow. But for quite some time, even as I recognized that something fundamental in my environment had changed, I kept questioning myself. Even as I *knew*, my brain started speaking over my heart. "I'm overreacting. I'm being too sensitive. Other people seem to be doing okay. Why can't I just deal?"

In reality, other people were *not* doing okay. They were just a bit better at adapting to the new climate, or they didn't show signs of stress initially. That didn't make them stronger than me. It also didn't make them less authentic for being able to adjust to a drastic climate change. Their own Essential Natures were more conducive to adaptation. Maybe they were dandelions! Some adapted as far as they could, and ended up moving on, as they ultimately couldn't continue to thrive in the new climate. As for me,

I left one of my favorite jobs ever—one I thought I would stay in for many more years—and I resigned.

Leaving that inhospitable climate didn't mean that I immediately put down new roots and started flowering. It took me years to adapt to my new ecosystem, even though I knew it was where I belonged. It took a bit of time to work out the details—all the issues that we'll explore in the next chapters: my new root system and nourishment, my pollinators in this new ecosystem, and the gifts that I could offer in my new life role.

So the question for you, if you find yourself recognizing that you're not in your optimal Thrivability Zone: adapt or move?

It's not always a one-or-the-other choice. It is more like a gradual shift, as we often start adapting to climate change before we realize we are. Remember, all organisms try to acclimate as an initial survival response. As a gardener, I can tell you that plants rarely succumb suddenly if they're in the wrong zone—unless there's frost. That's the death knell. But otherwise, they often use everything in their power to continue living where they are planted. I think we do the same as humans. It's *hard* to move away from life as we know it, so it's often a question of just surviving versus thriving.

Now that you've started exploring the aspects of Essential Nature that inform your Thrivability Zone and feelings of belonging, the sections below are designed to help you glean the important elements (Harvest the Fruit) and reflect on ways that the concepts can help you expand and grow (Plant the Seeds). You will find these sections at the conclusion of each chapter.

Next we'll consider how you create and manage your energy. We'll use the lens of the two most impactful conditions for the growth of plants. Light (the amount of sun a plant living outdoors needs to grow to its potential, flower, and set seed) and site (the attributes of where it's planted, including soil moisture) are the most crucial considerations once a plant is living in the correct zone. And while these needs aren't necessarily rigid requirements, lacking a requisite amount of both light and moisture eventually compromises a plant beyond healing. The same can be said for humans.

Key Takeaways — Harvest the Fruit:

- **Hardiness zones are about survival, not superiority.** A plant that can't handle zone 7 winters isn't "worse"—it simply belongs somewhere else. Same for humans: Your needs aren't a character flaw; they're part of your Essential Nature.

- **Thriving depends on the whole ecosystem**—soil, light, humidity, pollinators, and neighboring plants. For humans, our Thrivability Zone includes relationships, culture, values, pace, support, and the microclimates of daily life.

- **Cold is the make-or-break factor for plants because winter can kill.** In humans, "winter" can look like being frozen out, unsupported, isolated, or constantly bracing for impact.

- **Belonging includes both external inclusion and internal "rightness."** You can be welcomed—and still feel like a palm tree in Iceland. That internal mismatch matters.

- **Adaptation is an option, but it has a cost.** Humans can survive in less-than-ideal climates through strategies, resilience, boundaries, and communication—but surviving isn't the same as thriving.

- **When the climate changes, the question becomes: adapt, move, or both.** Life events can shift our entire environment. Sometimes you adjust your pot size. Sometimes you relocate your roots. Often it's a continuum—adapting first, then moving (internally or externally) when you reach your maximum tolerance.

Reflection Questions — Plant New Seeds:

- Where in your life do you feel the strongest sense of alignment and belonging—and where do you feel a mismatch or strain that limits your growth?

- What does your unique "plant tag" tell you about what you need to thrive (people, pace, stimulation, solitude, structure, creativity, consistency), and how well are those needs being met right now?

- What, if anything, needs to change—within you or in your environment—so you can grow to your full height and width in this season of your life?

How do you protect and renew your energy?

"The secret to life is to put yourself in the right lighting. For some it's a Broadway spotlight, for others, a lamplit desk."

— Susan Cain

"When life gets too intense, find your shade and feel secure."

— Frida Kahlo

Remember that "backward" girl I was as a child? I know now that part of my reluctance to open up and engage was an attempt to protect my energy, to keep myself shielded from people and situations that felt overwhelming. But that pronouncement from my mom—said in a way that suggested an apology or a feeling of embarrassment—became a core aspect of my identity, as judgments from parents often do. And it was directly connected to a feeling of shame. Even if it was inadvertent, I received a message that my way of being in the world and of managing my feelings was wrong or flawed.

It took me years to recognize that my need for solitude—my introversion—is not weird or even pathological. It is simply part of my Essential Nature—I need to create some distance from people and situations that feel too intense. It is more than managing my social exposure, stimulation, and level of interaction, although those were the outcomes. Truly, solitude is a form of emotional and spiritual nourishment for me—a source of joy.

Those times when I felt like the world was too bright and I needed some type of cool shelter, I instinctively found it through turning into myself. And it was that coolness and detachment that energized me and brought me back to myself.

Varying needs for connection are normal, and even when we try to puzzle out our own needs, it can feel baffling! We need both community and connection, as well as space and solitude, to manage the energy we expend to handle stressors. Sometimes, social situations can create stress.

We often refer to our reaction within social relationships in terms of *introversion* or *extraversion*. Some people may consider themselves ambiverts—the middle of the road between the two. However, introversion/ extraversion is a continuum—even if we fall in the middle, our need for connection or solitude can vary from day to day—or even minute to minute. The terms are sometimes misunderstood or worse, assigned value based on societal rules. In western culture, we tend to value extraversion—being outgoing, the life of the party. Introverts are often characterized as weird, quirky, or awkward.

While there are various definitions of these traits, in the mental health world we tend to think of these as ways to measure where we focus our thoughts and experiences, and how we use that preference to guard our energy, as well as to renew it. For example, introversion tends to be characterized by introspection—a tendency to focus on one's inner thoughts and ideas. Extroverts—you guessed it—tend to focus outward, drawing energy from other people and situations. Neither is better than the other.

The key, as with everything, is to know your own needs and accept them as valid—know what is on your plant tag! Because these are just terms to describe human photosynthesis.

Simply put, *photosynthesis* is the process by which a plant uses light to create energy. As part of the beauty of the ecosystem, it does this by converting carbon dioxide—which mammals, including humans, exhale—into energy the plant uses to grow and reproduce. And, maybe the most amazing part, the byproduct of this process is oxygen, the very element humans need to survive!

Obviously humans don't photosynthesize in a literal sense. But we do take what is part of our environment—other people, our community, and our workplace—and use our own resources to convert it to energy. And ideally, this allows us to inject something positive of ourselves—our own unique oxygen—back into that environment.

And just as humans have a scope of preferences for social connection and energy focus, plants have a continuum of preferences for the amount of sun and shade they need to live their best lives—to execute optimal photosynthesis.

The same way that declaring someone an introvert or an extrovert misses the nuance in the variability of how this personality trait affects them, plants can't simply be divided into shade-loving and sun-loving plants, if gardeners truly want a thriving garden. Yet, I often hear people simplify this aspect of plants. And we are often guilty of that in our human world. We rely on social media personalities or one source of information to inform our idea of what is acceptable.

Light is a non-negotiable for most plants. Just like a plant in a dark room will grow toward the meager glow of a single candle flame, humans—even those needing high levels of solitude—can't thrive in the total absence of connection. We produce a hormone that functions like a chemical messenger of love. The cuddle hormone, *oxytocin*, creates the desire for humans to connect, and it also surges during childbirth, where it has numerous roles, including facilitating the bonding process of mother and baby.

Conversely, too much light can also threaten a plant's ability to survive. Twenty-four hours of hot, unrelenting sunshine would over-tax a plant in the same way trying to maintain a fully external focus—no down-time— would severely compromise even the most gregarious extrovert. Relying on outside relationships for all our needs undermines our ability to fully develop independence and self-reliance.

The need for connection varies from person to person, like site preferences for plants. While even species that prefer dense shade, like certain varieties of ferns (*Polypodiopsida*), hostas (*Hosta*), and lungwort (*Pulmonaria*), would not survive in the total absence of light, even 30 minutes of direct sun can cause these plants to begin wilting. This illustrates the difference between filtered or dappled sunlight and full-on, blinding sunshine.

The *Geranium biokovo* is an example of the impact of filtered versus direct sunlight. It has a lush, mounding habit, and its flowers look like darling fairies. Every year I swear it's going to die in the few short hours that the sun hits it directly; it looks like it's gasped its last breath. But once the sun passes by and it's in evening shade, it's like, "Nothing to see here." It's totally stressed for about three hours out of the day, then it gets what it wants again and it recovers. However, I know that daily physical wilting, then recovery, comes at a cost for the plant, because it relies on the gardener (me, in this case) to put it where it will thrive. Until then, it adapts to survive the best it can and, in the case of the geranium, to produce flowers. (Ironically, this geranium was planted in a less than ideal location because I believed the tag that was attached to the pot when I purchased it.)

Geranium biokovo

This is not the first time I believed the label, planting something in the exact sun/shade location described on the tag, only to have it struggle to thrive. As humans, we love the neatness and the clear, black-and-white of labels. However, the attributes of a label—for plants *and* for humans—are decided by observers. Thus they are often inaccurate. *You* get to decide what's on your plant tag. My mom wanted to write "backward" on mine. But I knew that wasn't accurate, and eventually, I decided to determine the site where I thrived.

When you think about your ideal environment for renewing or creating energy, what do you sense is right, based on your Essential Nature? Would you love living in a rainforest under dense overgrowth, like a fern, where you rarely get more than a beam of sunlight for a few minutes? Or are you a desert plant, like a cactus, loving the sharp, brilliant sun with only the cool night to rest or the rare storm to create shadows?

The jungle fern and the desert cacti are clearly opposite ends of the spectrum. There *are* people who truly prefer one of these situations, but they, too, are on the far ends of a continuum. Just as there are very few plants that thrive in these conditions, there aren't many of us who want to live in an environment of constant connection or continual isolation. Incidentally, cacti absorb the carbon dioxide they need to convert energy at night, by opening their *stomata* (pores). Completing this process during the cooler temperatures of nighttime helps them to conserve water. This helps illustrate that even plants that were made to endure the harshest, hottest sunlight have built-in mechanisms to optimize their thriving by giving them a break from the most intense environmental conditions. This is an example of why it's a bit simplistic to talk of humans as one of two extremes: introverted or extroverted. Human needs are as nuanced and varied as the need for light is in the plant world.

Even the various plants within a species each have their own ratio of sun and shade. One of my most beloved shade plants, *Heuchera*, comes in an amazing array of foliage hues. Every single one in my garden is stressed by even an hour or two of too much sun, becoming crispy and brown—except for one. This majestic variety—maroon leaves with magenta spots scattered across them—thrives in eight hours of full sun. This plant reminds me every year not to stereotype. Even the name sunflower (*Helianthus)* is misleading, as there are varieties that tolerate shade, like the woodland sunflower (*Helianthus divaricatus*) and the swamp sunflower (*Helianthus angustifolius*).

Plants that prefer shade typically have leaves that are a darker green and contain more *chlorophyll*, the pigment they use to convert light to energy. This is what makes them more efficient at creating energy from less light. But it is also what makes them more vulnerable to too much light. (As with many things in life, our strength is our weakness.) When we think of this in terms of humans, we may have more sensitivity to overload from social interaction or exposure to the energy (heat) of others. We simply have more chlorophyll, if you will.

As you're reading this, you might be identifying with the need to move away from stimulation as your best means of emotional energy renewal. Maybe you're thinking, "Yes, I am *totally* a fern!" But what if this just *doesn't* feel aligned with what you know of yourself? What if you thrive the most in the situations that make a fern-person run for shade? Perhaps you instinctively move toward people and situations that feel warm or even hot. You are living your best life when you can experience consistent connection.

Fern

If you love lively crowds, noisy parties, the crush of concert-goers, or weekends of late nights and active days, you would be a sun-loving plant! You love the hot intensity of connection, and you need it to energize. Long periods of shade, including solitary activities, don't give you enough light to convert into energy. In fact, lack of connection may make you feel out-of-sorts or even depressed. And that means you can't bring as much of yourself—your oxygen—to the world because you don't have enough of what you instinctively and naturally need to be at your best.

You might be lavender (*Lavandula*). Lavender needs hot, bright sunlight. When it's sited correctly, it will grow full, fragrant foliage and send up straight, sturdy flower spikes. In cooler summers, it loves the extra warmth from being planted next to a brick or stone wall or having white stones covering the soil so it can absorb the reflected heat. And when you have these optimal conditions, you are one of the most useful and beloved sources of herbal remedies.

Or, maybe you want to live with a bit more pizzazz—you're a coneflower! Their blooms range from hot pink to white, cayenne, and even soft lime green. Most of them aren't as picky when it comes to lean, hot soil as lavender is. Coneflowers often spread throughout the garden, and they have their own medicinal properties stored mostly in their roots. Plus their seeds provide winter food for finches.

Rarely are plants sited perfectly, even by the most experienced gardener. This is where adaptation comes in. If a plant gets more sun than it prefers, it can actually get sun-burnt! Their foliage becomes bleached, their leaf margins scorch, or burn spots appear on the leaves. However, if they are moved into protective shade, they can recover—if it's done soon enough.

Likewise, after navigating through situations of too much social exposure or stimulation and finally enjoying a period of solitude, I can feel my stomach relax and the tightness in my chest ease. In situations where there is no human equivalent of shade or an opportunity to honor the needs of my Essential Nature, I can navigate through them by managing my reserves, much in the same way that plants can respond to protect themselves. However, depending on the situation, recovery time will vary.

When I was young, I instinctively moved out of a situation that felt scorching as soon as possible, hiding behind my mom or going to the cool, dark forest. In my child's mind, I didn't reason through my choice. I reacted instinctively, from my Essential Nature, and moved to an environment where I could calm myself and recharge. I was finding my optimal conditions to photosynthesize!

My strategies evolved, once I accepted my tendency as natural, and I recognized the adaptation I was making to manage something outside of my control. When we acknowledge our instinct for self-protection is part of our nature, we can work *with* it instead of trying to cope in ways that aren't natural to us.

Plants are masters of adaptation. When the light is too intense for shade plants, they compensate for extra-efficient chlorophyll by curling their leaves to limit the surface area that is exposed to the sun. They may also simply droop, wilt, or turn their leaves away from the brightness to get some relief.

But that's not their only option—they can transfer the energy absorbed by their chlorophyll into *carotenoids*, which can offload some of that energy as heat. They may opt for *transpiration*, the process of releasing water vapor through *stomata* (small pores on the leaf surface), to cool down and regulate their temperature—the plant equivalent of blowing off steam. Plants have many ways of adjusting to overwhelming environments, and we often marvel at their adaptability. Yet when you choose novel means to manage or protect your energy, you may worry you will be judged as weak or weird. Instead, try to embrace your uniqueness in the same way we do for the wondrous array of adaptations in nature.

Perhaps the most amazing acclimation ability of all is that plants can produce their own sunscreen in the form of *flavonoids*, especially under UVB radiation stress, and some species of plants develop reflective hairs called *trichomes*, which can act as a sunscreen and also help reduce water loss.

Plants—rooted in a stationary location and without our human ability to reason and use logic—have wonderful and effective means to manage a situation that literally threatens their survival. They don't debate and question themselves. And they certainly don't gaze across the lawn at the sunflowers or lavender absorbing the sunlight like happy chlorophyll sponges and question their own need for relief or worse, wonder why they can't be more like the extroverted coneflower and fret that they aren't as amazing as the sun-loving plants. You, my friend, may do all those things if you compare your coping strategies or instinctual needs to those of your friends, family, or social media influencers, that subtly or blatantly suggest there is one right way of being.

A huge benefit of being human is that we can move toward what we need. We can lean into or away from situations that are sapping our energy. Just as I recognized that I need to find solitude to re-energize, we can manage many situations in our lives to optimize our Essential Nature. You may prefer to build flagging energy by leaning *toward* people—getting more involved in your community or joining social groups. Truly knowing and learning to honor your Essential Nature informs your focus.

Further, our life is an array of environments, which means we have varying needs, depending on the situation. We may not have the same need for shade (space and distance) or sun (connection) in relationships where we have evolved with someone, say a sibling or a partner with whom we are in a long-term relationship. We feel safe, and we have adapted to the circumstances—the *biodiversity* and *mutualism*—that exists in the environment, if those relationships are healthy. For example, the biodiversity of our human lives includes the rhythms of existence, and the people, schedules, and situations that create our unique ecosystem. Mutualism is the symbiosis in our relationship: Much like the bee and the flower both benefit from the act of pollination, we have a give-and-take to our close relationships that benefit each person.

Our work or social life may require a different need for distance and shade than our family life—or vice versa. Even vacations may make us feel like we have momentarily transformed from a hosta to a heat-loving lavender plant.

Life circumstances change all the time, even subtly. Plants respond differently to light based on the season, for example. My *Geranium biokovo* doesn't wilt dramatically until the full heat of summer. During the spring warm-up, the sunlight isn't as intense, since the sun is at a lower angle in the sky. Sometimes it's the degree of light—or stimulation, in terms of people—that makes the difference in the way we manage our energy. When I'm at a party with a couple hundred people, you will find me, at some point, leaving and walking alone or simply sitting in a spot away from the fray. However, if I'm part of a more intimate gathering with close friends, I'm typically doing 50 percent of the talking. Different sites, different needs.

Just like plants, our lives have seasons that impact our ability to create emotional energy from our environment. Take holidays, for example. If you celebrate Christmas or any other holiday that brings family and friends together to an increased frequency, it can create a mini-environmental crisis of the human kind. It can feel like global warming is slowly consuming your life—hot and inescapable.

It's rare that we don't eventually acclimate to all of our life changes, provided we acknowledge and honor the needs of our Essential Nature when it comes to emotional energy management. This starts with simply (but perhaps not easily) accepting your needs as valid and either building into life more of what charges your batteries or lessening some of what depletes you—weathering the situational ebbs and flows of life. And they aren't all negative.

Often we underestimate the need to adjust to *eustress*—"good" stress brought on by events that are socially characterized as positive. We have new relationships, and we bring babies into the world—yes, blessings—but also situations that change the site where we are growing. And then there are losses, changes to jobs, and even national political policies that can impact our neighborhoods and communities. Loss can feel like clouds are covering the sun. It can create a feeling of cold detachment and a yearning for more connection (or less, depending on your Essential Nature) than we typically desire.

Change is a constant, just like no two summers are the same for plants. What if a tree falls down in a storm and the ferns, happily settled and thriving in their colony underneath it, suddenly find themselves exposed to the brutal sun with no protection? Conversely, what will the coneflowers do when the maple tree that was planted a few years ago finally attains a height that creates longer shade, robbing them of the amount of sun they need to grow to their fullest potential?

When the environment around a plant changes drastically, their salvation is in both their resilience and their ability to adjust to the changes. Plants that have a limited ability to adapt or a more narrow band of conditions for survival are much more vulnerable than those that are more hardy. Perhaps those ferns can slow their growth and adjust their photosynthesis until the flora around them attains enough height to again provide shade. And the coneflower may grow longer stems to reach the edge of the light where they can drop their seeds and endure through natural propagation.

Neither of these strategies are instantaneous. While plants recognize immediately the need to regulate their growth, the actual adapting is a long-game strategy. In the same way, the sooner we acknowledge changes in our environment, the better we can modify our mindset and our behaviors to acclimate in a way that works best with the ways we manage our energy.

At one point in my career, I took a job that was vastly different from my previous ones. In those first few weeks on the job, I nearly fled the building at lunch time, my chest tight to the point that I was short of breath. I drove to a nearby mall, and simply sat in my car, eating my lunch and reading a book. By the time I needed to return to work, the tightness eased, and I was ready to re-engage. A week or so after starting my new position, a colleague commented to me, "Maybe you should actually have lunch with some of the staff and get to know people." I remember the dread that curled into my stomach as I felt my cheeks grow hot. But by then, I had started understanding myself. I had done a great deal of adapting in various situations, and I was able to recognize that my need to adjust in my own way was valid. So I just smiled and told her that my lunch reprieves were temporary.

Bottom line: Nature will work to find balance, to create homeostasis. Humans are no different.

However, there are times when an environment is simply inhospitable or even toxic, and no amount of flexibility can fully overcome the stressors. I know what happens to plants that are robbed of their need for light or shade over and over. They can only adapt so far. First, they will try to grow in a way that doesn't benefit their true nature, as we've discussed previously. Amazing resilience. But if it goes on too long, future thriving is at risk.

As part of nature, humans can suffer the same fate. In the face of the chronic stress of poverty, or environmental toxins, or a dysfunctional family, we will often stay small or we will reach and stretch ourselves so thin that we are unrecognizable. Like plants struggling to survive, we will stop flowering because that process takes incredible energy. This is a crisis, because it can compromise the way we nurture and support the next generation. Finally, our leaves will be too weakened to create energy from the light of our environment, whether it is scorching us or we feel cold and detached. And our greatest gift—to impact the world around us and leave a legacy, to put our unique gifts of oxygen back into the world—will no longer be an option.

What a price we pay when we convince ourselves that our environment isn't important and our true, deep Essential Nature can be compromised!

Honoring what you instinctively strive for is paramount to respecting your true nature. If you're a fern—you thrive with lots of solitude, but still need some filtered sunlight—you don't need to try to be a sun-loving coneflower. And you most assuredly don't need to be a sunflower!

Everything plants do is in the pursuit of survival—if not of itself individually, then as a species.

And the job where I fled to the sanctity of my car at lunchtime? You may be surprised to know that I ended up being promoted into a position where I ran staff trainings, organized huge institutional events, and spoke to rooms full of people. How could I go from fleeing to my car to being instrumental in the day-to-day functioning of the company? Taking time to make the adjustments to my new surroundings in a way that honored my Essential Nature allowed me to put down roots, to connect to my organization and create relationships. I also learned where I was able to get the nourishment I needed: supportive supervisors, respectful collaboration, and encouragement to grow into new opportunities.

Even when we move plants to *more* hospitable environments, they need time to establish new roots and find means of nutrients. Short term impact for long term gains. There's so much we can learn from plants' ability to maximize their own opportunities to build healthy roots for connection and nourishment. Let's explore that next.

Key Takeaways — Harvest the Fruit:

- **Messages we receive in childhood about being "too much," "not enough," or "backward" often shape identity.** When our natural ways of protecting and managing energy are judged, we may come to believe we are flawed rather than simply unique.

- **Your need for solitude or connection is part of your Essential Nature**, not a problem to fix. Introversion, extraversion, and everything in between are natural variations in how humans renew energy. Solitude can be as nourishing and life-giving as community—just as shade is essential for some plants.

- **Energy needs exist on a continuum and change with context and season.** No one is purely a "fern" or a "sunflower" all the time. Our need for space or connection shifts based on relationships, environments, stress levels, and life seasons. What works in one setting may be draining in another.

- **Cultural bias and societal messages lead people to override their natural rhythms**—instead of honoring what actually helps them thrive. Extraversion is often praised, while sensitivity and introspection are misunderstood or minimized.

- **Adaptation is resilience—but it has limits.** Like plants, humans can adjust to less-than-ideal environments through coping strategies. But chronic exposure to environments that don't meet our core needs eventually compromises our ability to flourish, create, and "flower."

- **Managing emotional energy is a process that is unique to each of us.** Understanding what we need allows us to choose environments, routines, and recovery strategies that support us—without shame or comparison.

Reflection Questions — Plant New Seeds:

- What labels or identities about how you relate to people, energy, or emotion still shape how you see yourself—and which are ready to be rewritten?

- When you feel most restored (not just functional), what conditions are present—light, stimulation, solitude or connection—and how does your body signal that it's out of balance?

- Where are you adapting to survive rather than being truly aligned, and what small, practical shifts would help you feel more accurately sited in this season of life?

CHAPTER 3 ROOTS AND NUTRIENTS:

What sustains you?

*"People are like dirt. They can either nourish you
and help you grow as a person or they can stunt
your growth and make you wilt and die."*

— PLATO

*"You can't be a resource for others
unless you nourish yourself."*

— ALEXANDRA STODDARD

As humans, many qualities of our environment sustain us. Often, we think first of food, which is certainly a necessary component of survival and, yes, thriving, depending on what we consume. But our entire way of living can either support us or deplete us.

Our connections nurture us and allow times of joy. Just as plants have roots designed to bring them the nutrients needed for growth, humans have connections to people and life situations that bring us the sustenance we need to survive or, preferably, thrive. As we explored in the last chapter, our energy is connected to how we navigate our social relationships. We are literally wired to connect, and our physical bodies reinforce this through the release of oxytocin.

Nature itself is continually created and sustained by connection, through the ecosystem of pollination and communication between and among plants and insect species. But much of this support comes from below ground as well, from *mycorrhizal* (fungal) connections between elements in the soil that even help trees communicate through their roots!

As humans, we often simplify what we need to thrive, thinking only in terms of food and rest—both of which are obviously crucial—and paying less attention to the myriad of ways we get nourishment from our environment. Though we recognize the importance of food, we may not understand our own unique nutrient needs, which are different from others, even those in our own family. And beyond the literal nutrition of food, we tend to downplay the impact of our environment's input—our soil.

Soil itself varies widely in terms of the components, the physical properties, and the layers or *horizons*. Growing plants that fully flourish—not only those that reach their ideal height, width, and mass, but that propagate and contribute positively to the ecosystem—means a gardener can't just plop them into the soil anywhere. As we've explored previously, the zone and light requirements are crucial. And hopefully you now recognize what that means for your own growth.

Let's dismantle some of the features of soil that impact plants, and start relating it to how we find nourishment. The first facet is understanding what truly sustains you, and that knowledge, as with most aspects of our thriving, comes right from your Essential Nature. It starts with your roots.

You have your own unique root system—ways in which you are connected to your environment, and how you communicate to get what you need. For example, you may be deeply committed to your community, like a *taproot* that runs far down into the soil, or you may have shallow and far-reaching *fibrous roots* that create more plentiful connections to others.

Let's start with the taproot, and the quintessential deep-rooted plant: the dandelion (*Taraxacum officinale*). Dandelions have quite a wide climate range, as you've learned. So I'm guessing there's a good chance you have encountered this plant either in your quest for a perfect lawn, a weedless garden, or a healthy diet. Dandelion leaves are packed with vitamins, minerals, and antioxidants. Maybe it's their amazing roots that pull nutrients from deep in the soil.

Dandelions are anchored to their environment. I need a small digging tool to get the entire taproot out of the ground when I'm weeding my flower beds. If I miss even a tiny part, there's a good chance it will regrow. But it takes a lot of energy to regrow in a spot where someone tried to eradicate you. Another dandelion superpower is that they aren't too concerned about where they are growing—they just make the best of it. They grow in the cracks of sidewalks. They are low maintenance and tenacious, for sure. However, that might not always serve their ultimate growth.

Let's think about that taproot. What might that look like in terms of human connection to our living situation? Is it similar to a person that was born, raised, and spent their entire life in the same town? We'd usually say that those people have some deep roots. But do you know how dandelions spread? Their fluffy seed heads are masters of propagation—and they can often germinate wherever they land. They dig deep, with no hesitation. They commit to staying and growing, no matter what might try to disrupt them. They are flexible in adapting to the nutrients that are there.

Are you someone who can go with the flow and adapt to wherever you land? What a great strength, right? But sometimes, it might not serve you. Do you fully commit, even if that means you might struggle? Think about what would happen if you planted yourself in the crack of a sidewalk. You'd get stepped on quite a bit. Or if you were emotionally uprooted or you had losses, like a job or a relationship, would you take your remaining connection—your severed taproot—and use all your energy to grow again, in the same soil, the same life situation?

The vast majority of plants have a fibrous root system—quite different from a taproot as a mechanism for pulling in nutrients and moisture from the soil. Unlike that single prominent taproot, fibrous roots are clusters of roughly the same size that grow out of the bottom of the plant stem into the soil. Because fibrous roots lack a long, anchoring taproot, the plants that have this type of root aren't as deeply connected to the ground as separate plants.

Let me explain: We often find dandelions growing in isolation from other dandelions, either as a solitary interloper in the managed garden bed or as scattered sentries throughout a suburban lawn. Alternatively, the strength of fibrous roots is that they are a system, which means that their smaller, branching roots spread out into the soil and intertwine with roots of other plants. Their strength is in numbers. Grasses have fibrous roots. If you've ever tried to single out one grass plant and pull it out, you know that it's bringing some friends along. And they will all resist you as one single unit.

So while a dandelion goes deep and connects with commitment, it's kind of a solo act. Grasses, on the other hand, favor community and connection. While they may not have the advantage of pulling nutrients from deep in the soil, they can spread out and expand to pull nutrients from closer to the surface. They would benefit more from applied fertilizers, for example. Plants with fibrous roots can't land somewhere and dig in, like a dandelion can do with its seeds. Grasses tend to be steady and consistent, spreading into new areas (like flower beds) much to the chagrin of fastidious gardeners. And like the tenacious dandelion, grass will certainly grow into cracks in sidewalks and driveways that are adjacent to a lawn. But when it gets stepped on, it spreads the stress over all its grass buddies with their intertwined roots—they share the burden of difficult situations.

While even taproots have some side rootlets that grow off of the main root, fibrous roots put their eggs in more baskets. If you find support and sustenance from your family, co-workers, or any group with which you have a shared mission or shared affection, the idea of growing more independently might feel wrong for your Essential Nature. While damage to others with whom you have interconnected roots affects you, too, perhaps the idea of knowing you are part of a mutually dependent community is a requirement for you to feel grounded—to feel a sense of belonging—as you do in your Thrivability Zone.

Adventitious roots are one of the most hopeful types of roots. They can form on intact plant stems, simply as a means to connect the plant more securely to the ground. Having grown up in a largely agricultural area of Pennsylvania, I often saw adventitious roots on the tallest, leafiest corn plants. Specifically called *brace roots*, they were tough and sturdy, growing out of the stem about six inches or so above ground, and disappearing into the earth like a circle of fleshy ropes.

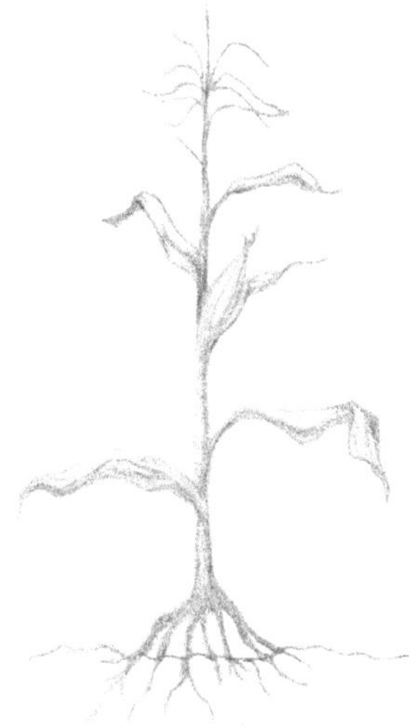

Corn plant with brace roots

Injury to a stem is another situation in which adventitious roots will grow. This proclivity is often utilized when propagating plants. If you've ever taken a cutting of a houseplant and put it into water, its tendency to sprout roots is an instance of adventitious roots. This is a great way to propagate succulents: Simply break off a fleshy leaf and put it directly into the soil. Look after it properly and it will develop roots.

In the case of plant cuttings, roots will grow on the severed end of the cutting if it is given the correct conditions—submerging in water or dipping in a rooting powder and planting directly into a potting medium. If tended properly, each cutting becomes an independent plant with minimal damage to the mother plant.

But not all plants can develop roots in this manner. In the case of lavender and strawberries, roots will form where it bends down and connects to the soil. This is called *layering*. Although it is still connected to the mother, once it forms its own roots, it will be a fully independent plant. Kind of like giving our children support to develop their own resources to live fully on their own.

In the same way as roots develop when there is injury to the plant, humans sometimes need to adapt and find new support when we experience trauma or anything that injures our body, mind, or spirit. Survival universally requires new growth.

If we lose someone we love, that source of nourishment is gone. Or if we have a physical challenge, we compensate by finding other means to support our new needs or gain additional assistance. Our ways of adapting are based on not only what is gone, but how we lost it.

However, if we try to move on and bury the pain or pretend we (and life) are the same as before ("Nothing to see here!"), we run the risk of developing a callus on that part of our heart.

In the plant world, a tree, for example, sustains an injury when a limb is severed. Often, the tree will develop a collar around the injury to protect it. Ironically, this is called a *callus,* the equivalent of human emotional scabs. Eventually, that protection hardens into *woundwood*—tougher tree tissue that covers up the damage. Other trees may react to cutting or pruning by sending up tiny new branches, called *suckers*. This is an attempt to compensate for the loss of leaves and their mechanism of photosynthesis. They need to recoup their losses.

These plants evolved to cope in these ways. Humans, however, often compromise their mental, emotional, and physical health when they try to simply cover their trauma. While it might *feel* relieving in the short term—an open wound is painful, right? We aren't trees. We can't pretend our heart is made of wood and that we can simply patch it up with woundwood!

This is where adventitious roots—ways of growing and learning from trauma—increase our resilience and our overall health. Remember that connection is literally part of our hormones, our endocrine system, in the form of oxytocin. Reaching out to connect—to other people, to a therapist, to soul-sustaining nature—brings in new sources of nourishment from the very site of injury.

Feeling and even showing the impact of suffering is healthy and normal. Too often, we believe that if we're strong, we should just bounce back. We may look at others' stories on social media and feel shame that we can't just move on and focus on the future.

Experiencing trauma or even impactful childhood socialization (limiting narratives, bullying, or harsh parental judgment) can act like stuck energy in the body. In the same way that a plant will send its own agents of healing to the site of a physical injury, I have seen countless instances of emotional distress manifesting as a bodily ailment.

For example, in 2005, I felt a lump at the base of my neck. I clearly remember the russet-orange wool sweater I was wearing, which caused me to scratch my neck along the itchy collar. And I felt it. It was a smooth lump the size of a large pea. A tiny sliver of ice pierced my heart, and I swear it skipped three beats.

I had a biopsy. Thyroid cancer. I mentally batted around numerous theories, because don't we always search for the "why" of our misfortunes? These musings included the fact that I grew up less than 10 miles downstream from Three Mile Island, the site of the worst nuclear near-disaster (depending who you ask) in the United States. Could *that* be the source of my cancer?

What I believe today is that cancer grew where my energy was stuck. As a girl, sharing my opinion wasn't always welcomed. As a young woman, the same was true. So when I learned that all of us have latent cancer cells in our bodies, it felt true to me that the continual swallowing of my opinions and keeping myself emotionally small and low maintenance somehow encouraged those malignant cells to grow.

When a plant suffers an injury or loses a main source of support, there are almost always obvious signs. The plant will show stress by wilting, failing to flower, or dropping leaves. Nature doesn't try to hide this, as that would simply create just one more stressor, right? When I tried to hide my Essential Nature, it "spoke up" in the only way it could.

Yet often when we are in a situation of high stress due to a change in our life, we not only believe that we need to act like everything is fine, but we also want to shelter our loved ones from being burdened by our challenges. We especially try to shield our children, if they are part of the equation.

We are made to adapt to loss by reaching out into our ecosystem and finding additional support. The initial stress will most certainly affect us in ways similar to how losing part of a root system will impact a plant—it cannot continue to do all the things it would normally do to fully branch out. The plant will go into survival mode while it grows new roots, and it will shut down functions that would require nutrients it can't obtain due to having fewer roots available to absorb minerals and moisture. It is focused on the most important task: maintaining life and developing a new means of getting what it needs. It is absolutely a programmed part of survival to struggle, slowly adapt, and grow new means of support, then gradually work to get back to thriving. Make no mistake: that plant will never be the same plant it was before it was injured. But if it can heal, it still has the ability to flourish.

That plant also doesn't use its precious energy worrying about what it could have been if this hadn't happened or whether it's really okay to reach out with new roots to access additional nourishment. In the same way, reaching into our environment to find new sustenance in the form of mental, emotional, and spiritual nourishment for ourselves is as imperative as sourcing medical help for our loved one's illness.

Yet we often have an inner dialogue arising from these situations. We may believe we can't or shouldn't burden others with our issues, while at the same time, those that care about us usually want to help. Being honest with your needs and requesting specific help, as well as being open to answering your loved one's questions, will make them stronger and more capable of coping with and responding to challenges of their own.

Normalizing that bad things sometimes happen, and that adapting is hard but necessary, is invaluable in living a well-adjusted life. Teach yourself and others to grow adventitious roots from injury or heartbreak, and find new sources of support and nourishment from your existing root structure.

Plants illustrate this lesson quite clearly—stress, when manageable, doesn't weaken our roots. Quite the opposite, in fact. When a child or a plant is young, that seems counterintuitive. However, I learned that lesson the hard way—and on a large scale.

For a decade, I was married to a small-scale vegetable and fruit farmer. We would tend dozens of trays of seedlings that would eventually be planted directly into the fields, including tiny shoots of tomato, pepper, and other assorted veggies. While germinating and starting their growth, these little guys were pampered: timed watering, strategic fertilizer, and grow lights on a schedule to mimic nature. They were given every advantage. But guess what would happen if we carried them directly to the field on the first hot day and planted them directly into the ground? They would die. Or if they didn't actually die, their growth would be compromised and their survival would require extra care, setting our harvest schedule back by weeks.

So what did we do to prepare those pampered seedlings for their new life outside? We transitioned them to an outdoor covered growing area, tempering the heat of the direct sun and conserving some of the moisture so they didn't dry out too fast. But that wasn't all: We also brushed our hand across those little green sprites several times a day to help them transition. Imagine living in a sheltered environment for your entire life, then all of a sudden walking outside and experiencing wind, unfiltered sun and, to add insult to injury, all the pests just waiting to eat you for lunch!

Nature knows that the world isn't kind, as a rule. And while there are amazing joys in life, the blows can be swift and brutal. So give young ones in your care all the preparation you can, because that is what will foster their resilience. The same is true for *you*. Any situation that requires adjustment, adaptation, or healing should include building your resources—bolstering your root system—so you can have the best foundation for new growth.

Saplings—adolescent trees—need time to grow and anchor their roots, so for their early life, they remain flexible so that they bend in the wind; they don't break. And the impact of wind helps the roots to grow deep to better anchor the tree. Like the corn plant sending out brace roots to anchor it more securely, tree roots grow in a way that will best connect them to the earth and bring in the nutrients they need as they expand into the unique and often expansive space they will inhabit in their ecosystem.

Okay, so there is one type of root I didn't mention yet. Plants like tulips (*Tulipa*), dahlias (*Dahlia*), potatoes, lilies (*Hemerocallis*), and crocus (*Crocus*) store much of their needed nutrients in a large, fibrous structure in the soil. These types of structures include *bulbs, tubers, rhizomes,* and *corms*. For purposes of our discussion, we don't need to differentiate, and I'll focus on true bulbs, including tulips and daffodils (*Narcissus*). Bulbs have small roots that draw nutrients and moisture in, but the main source of nutrition for the plant comes from the bulb itself. These plants typically have a short growing season, and as they die back after a few weeks, their leaves will continue to absorb carbohydrate nutrients as they turn yellow and dry up.

Having underground storage units allows for the unique growth and flowering of these spring plants. Based on the cycle of light and dark, bulbs recognize when the days are starting to lengthen, and it's time to send up their stems and leaves. They are often fast-growing, putting all that stored energy into robust growth and big, showy flowers. The roots then pull moisture and nutrients into the bulb to restore what was lost, and ultimately, when the foliage dies back and falls off, the bulb rests and continues to recharge for its amazing display next spring.

I often think about the unique way that bulbs access nourishment and spend much of their bloom cycle on rest and restoration—nearly eleven months of the year—when I work with clients who have autoimmune issues that require a great deal of sleep. I know that these clients, 75 percent of whom are women, often battle false narratives that can be as taxing as dealing with their health issues themselves. We live in a culture, especially in the West, where our worth is measured by how we push through challenges and prioritize productivity over rest. Yet in the plant world, I have never heard any judgment leveled at bulbs because they spend 90 percent of their year storing up energy for their amazing display of flowers.

So what if we think about people as tulips? Recognize that sometimes we need to get sustenance from a less common root system. We need to get nutrients from our environment when we feel strong enough, and we often store those precious nutrients for maximum output at the times when we need to show up and perform. What if we simply acknowledge each others' contributions without questioning why we present ourselves in a way that doesn't match the acceptable narrative?

We don't truly know what anyone else is dealing with, so judging how they manage their energy is moot. And if you identify with the bulb's style of sustenance, yet you have an inner critic that discounts your unique need to build energy through rest and specific means of support, allow yourself to recognize what it takes for you to bloom. Honor your Essential Nature and fully be the tulip that you are meant to be.

Roots are one half of the equation when it comes to what sustains you. The roots are the mechanism, the natural tendency you have to access what you need. The other half of the equation is the nutrients that are in the soil where you were planted.

Generally, plants need 17 nutrients for normal growth. They obtain some from the air and water and others from the soil. I would venture to guess you could brainstorm 17 ways you, as a human, find support or nourishment from your environment. This includes food, of course, but also key relationships, hobbies, vocations and vacations, and any other endeavors that add joy. In the case of plants, of those 17 nutrients, six are considered macronutrients.

For us, macronutrients in our food are carbohydrates, fats, and protein. We need all three, and none of them are bad in their essential form. Similarly, most topical fertilizers will focus on three plant nutrients: nitrogen, phosphorus, and potassium.

So let's first think about how we sustain ourselves physically with our food. The food that best sustains our thriving is as unique as the ratio of nutrients that plants need. Although we can find a diet that will sing the praises of one human macronutrient and malign another, the truth about nutrition is much more nuanced. Most of us prefer clear guidelines and tend to feel overwhelmed and confused when we try to make our own choices about what is best to eat.

This book isn't the forum to discuss the intricacies of gut health and its connection to every single aspect of overall wellness, but I will mention a few universal facts. First, we are all unique as far as what foods will best sustain us, while still recognizing that we can prioritize specific nutrients.

While the nutritional impact of each of the three macronutrients has been misunderstood at some point—in my 20s and 30s, fat was considered the devil—we truly do need to consume all three. It is the quality and composition of those macronutrients that have the impact.

Just as plants growing in soil that is too lean or doesn't offer the needed nutrients will show signs of stress—yellow leaves, lack of flowering, wilting stems or even death—humans lacking the required nutrients eventually will too. We are just better at overlooking—or ignoring—early signs.

Expanding beyond food to the life choices that sustain or deplete us, let's consider Maslow's Hierarchy of Needs. These include physiological needs (food, air, water), safety, human connection, achievement/self-identity, and self-actualization. Maslow considered that we function based on what we most need at any point. For instance, it would be difficult to earn a promotion at work (achievement) if we did not first have access to basic needs like food and water. Overall, we can certainly get through a day if we're hungry, but if we live in poverty and are chronically undernourished, achievement is not only much harder, but we will likely care less about it.

If we are growing in an environment that isn't compatible with our most needed nutrients, we may need to amend our soil or find support. Let's look at how plants do this.

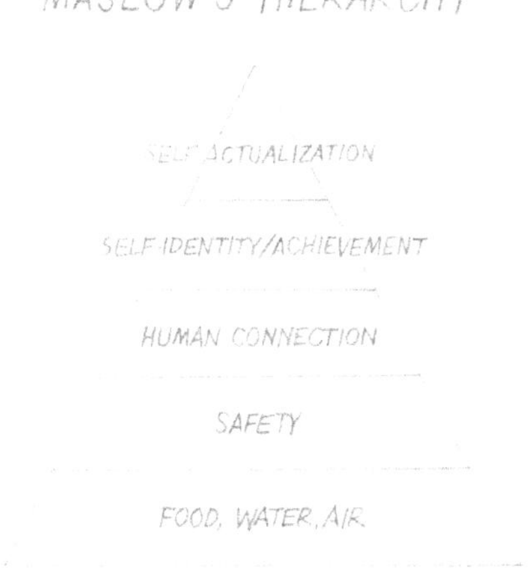

Nitrogen, one of the three plant macronutrients, is present in the atmosphere, but isn't accessible to plants in that form. There are specific plants—beans, for example—with bacteria living in nodules on their roots that convert nitrogen to ammonia for the plant's use. This is quite a useful process for neighboring plants who need the nitrogen but don't have the means to create the symbiotic relationship with the microorganisms in the way beans can. The bean roots host the bacteria that make the soil more nutritious for all the plants.

Now you aren't a bean, but there's certainly something we can learn from them. Where in your life do you have a symbiotic relationship? One example might be your career—you get paid in exchange for work. But symbiosis—a mutually beneficial relationship—is (hopefully) a characteristic of all your important relationships.

Novice gardeners often make the mistake of thinking *more is more* when it comes to fertilization. We can amend the soil to help plants reach their ultimate form and flowering, but the trick is that the ratio of the three macronutrients not only varies by plant, but by season. The scarcity or excess of a nutrient affects the foliage, flowering, and fruiting. In human terms, a lack or excess of nourishment may be reflected in our ability to show up prepared to make the most of our day and in our ability to bring our gifts to the world.

If a plant is growing near a bean plant, we know that it will have a nitrogen source. We can't see that symbiosis happening underground, so we may add more nitrogen, thus stressing the plant. When assessing your own nourishment, look for signs of stress. It's important to take a 360-degree view, to focus on how you look and feel physically and how you are managing your emotions, your cognitions, and your spirit.

It's rare for us—or a plant—to have the correct amount of every nutrient we need. When we think about food, we may simplify this, but trust me when I say that the foods that sustain you will not be the exact same as those that nourish someone else. Our gut is the center of everything. Our vagus nerve, the highway to physiological regulation, runs from our gut to our brain, informing it of the state of our entire body. Although sugars and saturated fats have deleterious health effects for all of us, how much they affect us and to what degree they will lead to serious health concerns will vary. We have all heard the stories of the centenarian that claims she tosses back a whiskey each evening before bed. Believe me, if that's true, she is a rare exception.

More specifically, for every person who can consume dairy or eat tomatoes, there is another for whom those foods will create inflammation. Starting with food that addresses your specific hormonal and metabolic situation is foundational, and within those parameters, choosing food that is as close to nature as possible is key. Just as drinking water treated with chemicals is less optimal for plants than rainwater, prioritizing organic and real foods over processed and packaged food will help us, as humans, thrive.

After satisfying our immediate physiological needs, we consider safety. In addition to the many examples we've already discussed, a threat to a plant results in adaptations to ensure survival. This means flourishing is not even on the agenda—the main objective is to ward off the threat.

However, the idea of "safety" will vary for each of us. In the case of toxic plants, they have an immediate advantage against pests versus the row of tantalizing, vulnerable new lettuce shoots. Healthy plants, overall, are less vulnerable, since a robust plant can withstand more munched leaves from hungry caterpillars and other larvae.

When you think of "safety," what do you consider? Perhaps you have cultivated resilience or, like a robust plant, you have a higher tolerance for risk. If you tend to focus narrowly on physical or financial safety, you may be risk averse, so you will put more protections in place, like lower-risk investments or extra password protections—the equivalent of erecting a fence to keep the bunnies away from those lettuce seedlings.

However, too much focus on one level of the hierarchy—in this case, safety—can be a detriment to reaching self-actualization—aka thriving. For example, on our organic farm, we often used row covers—floating, gauzy material—to cover crops to protect them from frost (in the case of blossoming strawberries plants) or greedy insects (vulnerable new seedlings). But if we neglected to remove the row cover, the plants would fail to produce; they need to eventually be open and available to the insects and wind that will facilitate pollination. No pollination, no fruit. We need to leverage safety against allowing some risk to reap the reward.

If your Essential Nature yearns for safety above other achievements, recognize if there are life situations that have resulted in your limiting your experiences or abdicating a higher level of achievement or even joy. If this feels true for you, hang in there. We'll explore both plant and human options for protection in future chapters.

Once basic needs and safety are met, human connection comes next. As we've already discussed, connection is a crucial aspect of both a healthy organism and a vibrant ecosystem. Consider your connection style and whether you need to adjust your soil to get more or less of what you prefer.

The top tiers of the hierarchy are where we get into the territory of thriving. Much of the foundation—physiological needs, safety, and connection—are what we address when we allow our Essential Nature to direct our adaptations. Once we feel those aspects are in alignment with our nature, we are free to find a higher level of achievement.

Attaining a healthy self-identity is the top of the pyramid. And even when we do achieve it, it isn't a permanent state—there will always be challenges that will test us and compel us to adapt in new ways. If you think about your life to this point, has it ever been consistent? Have you *permanently* attained the apex of your life?

Instead of feeling discouraged when life requires you to adapt yet again, recognize that life fluidity—ebbs and flows—isn't failure. Just as harsh seasons challenge plants and they weather the storms in their own unique ways, when we recognize, honor, and live through our Essential Nature, it will become increasingly easier to find fulfillment and success in difficult times.

Next let's explore more about self-identity—specifically, achievement—as we look at what lessons plants can offer about blooming and sharing our gifts. But first, take a minute to consider the main points of roots and nutrients and consider how they impact your own growth.

Key Takeaways — Harvest the Fruit:

- **Humans are sustained (or depleted) by relationships**, safety, nourishment, and the broader conditions of their lives, just as plants are shaped by their soil, light, and root systems.

- **Connection is a biological and emotional necessity.** Humans are wired for connection through hormones like oxytocin, much as plants rely on pollination and underground fungal networks. Isolation isn't just uncomfortable—it's destabilizing.

- **We each have a unique way of accessing nourishment**—our own "root system." Some people thrive with deep, singular connections (taproots), others through wide networks and shared support (fibrous roots), and some develop new sources of support after loss or injury (adventitious roots). No one root style is superior.

- **When injury occurs, plants grow new roots or redirect energy to survive.** Humans must do the same by reaching outward for support, allowing pain to be seen, and finding new ways to receive nourishment rather than sealing wounds.

- **Manageable stress paired with adequate resources builds resilience** and deeper anchoring, like seedlings gradually exposed to the elements or young tree roots strengthened by wind.

- **Bulbs remind us that long periods of rest and restoration are not laziness** or failure, but essential preparation for future blooming— especially for those managing chronic illness, fatigue, or invisible burdens.

Reflection Questions — Plant New Seeds:

- If your life were soil, what is truly nourishing you right now—and what is quietly depleting or thinning your reserves?

- Where does your root system feel strong and supported, and where has it learned to adapt, seal over pain, or grow without enough nourishment?

- In this season, what does "thriving" realistically look like for you—and what one gentle adjustment would support you in rooting more deeply where you are or reaching for new nourishment?

CHAPTER 4 BLOOMTIME:

What are your gifts?

*"A flower does not think of competing with
the flower next to it. It just blooms."*

—Zen Shin

"Every flower blooms in its own time"

— Ken Petti

We all bring our own unique gifts to the world. Everyone makes an impact, and the world is a different place because we each live in it. As every plant has a specific season, shape, color, and length of time for flowering, humans each have their own individual ways of blooming.

Gardeners often choose plants based on the attributes of their flowers. I'm drawn to lush purples and bright pinks, while my husband loves the warm, bright colors of orange and fire-engine red. (This sometimes makes for a challenging landscape design palette, but I will happily rise to this challenge in exchange for his enthusiastic support of my hours-long explorations of garden centers.) While I mix flower shapes to increase interest in my garden beds—and I can't undersell dahlias and Shasta daisies (*Leucanthemum*) for embodying the quintessential "perfect" flower shape—I find I have a fondness for the fluffy wands of foamflower (*Tiarella*), and false spirea (*Astilbe*), as well as the spiky bedhead of bee balm (*Monarda*).

The bloom pattern of certain plants mirrors how we, as humans, give our own gifts to the world. Individual plants can create more or fewer flowers, depending on their energy and their need to pass their seeds into the world. Remember that the overarching goal of nature is procreation—ensuring the survival of species. It would seem then, that all plants would create as many blooms as possible, for as long as possible, right? Well, let's think about that in terms of energy.

There are situations where plants will adjust to crises in the environment. For example, as we explored before, a plant that is subjected to too much sun over an extended time period will likely sacrifice some processes to preserve its strength. When it continually wilts and recovers from too much sun each day, it taxes the plant's vitality. And the most energy-laden process for a plant is producing flowers, so it may need to limit blooms in order to utilize its finite strength to survive, perhaps conserving the moisture in its stems, for example.

In the same way, elements of your own human environment can tax your reserves, at times. You may need to adjust your most energy-depleting processes when this happens. Even in our most proficient endeavors—the gifts we give to the world—we are not able to produce or execute flawlessly or in equal measure every single day or week or year. This is true even when we manage the sun/shade aspect of emotional energy conservation and renewal.

We often know where we need to conserve our stamina when we encounter stressors, but then the reasoning part of our brain starts the outer comparison and the inner dialogue. We gauge others' activity to measure our own unique need to limit our output, our gifts, our flowers.

Beyond the life situations that impact our ability to bloom and share our gifts are our innate ways of giving ourselves to the world. While our society seems to want to define *productivity* as needing to be consistent and prolific, each of us contributes to the world based on our complex (and valid) Essential Nature.

The most uniquely spectacular flowers can be found on the corpse flower (*Amorphophallus titanum*). The blooms, which occur once every few years, are open for only 24 hours and can reach 12 feet tall in the wild. Most of these plants are housed at public gardens or conservatories, and people come from miles away to see them during the brief window when the rare bloom graces the world. The single bloom is the color of decaying meat and reeks of rotting flesh—hence the common name, corpse flower. The scent is engineered by nature to attract the perfect pollinators: carrion beetles and flesh flies. As they lay their eggs, convinced by their olfactory organs that this is the perfect food source for their young, they do the important collateral work of pollinating. There is so much that is fascinatingly disgusting about this flower, yet it is a source of many people's awe and adoration—mine included.

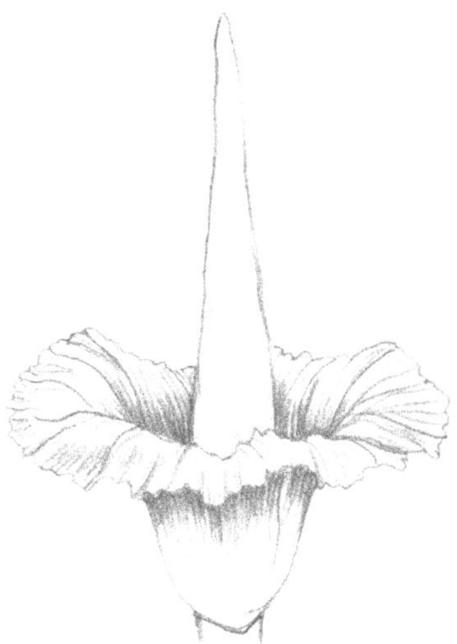

Corpse Flower (Amorphophallus titanum)

We can obviously recognize that the gargantuan size and the pungent scent place this plant in a class of its own, so we don't grouse that it may only bloom seven or eight times in our lifetime—we focus on its fascinating existence. We understand instinctively (or in-STINK-ively) that the flower takes a huge amount of energy to bloom. And just as the corpse flower's rare and singular accomplishment is a source of amazement for horticulturists and laypersons alike, there are people that produce one work of art or literature or music, have one child, or patent one invention. Each gift has value.

For example, the well-known author Sylvia Plath produced only one book, *The Bell Jar*. It's included in high school curricula in a vast number of schools, at least in the United States. In another field, Josephine Cochrane invented the dishwasher. That satisfies me—she can rest on her laurels. But overall, our society has unwritten "shoulds" for productivity. Although it's common now for someone to have one child, there used to be a profound sense of failure if a woman couldn't have more. If she was unable to conceive at all or, heaven forbid, she *chose* not to have children, the silent judgment often felt palpable.

For musicians, at least in the age before streaming services, the first question asked when a singer or a band dropped a new album was, "What are you planning for your next one?" Or when there was a popular show or a blockbuster movie, the question was, "Will there be a season two?" or "Will there be a sequel?"

In the world of music, one-hit wonders puzzle us: Surely if The Knack could produce "My Sharona" or Los Del Rio could make it big with "Macarena"—both of which hit number one on *Billboard* in the United States—they should be able to continue that success, right? I'm guessing at least one of those two songs is now forming an earworm in your brain— because the vast majority of us know one or both of those songs. That's a pretty amazing feat, right? Yet we tend to focus on why they couldn't repeat that success.

The world often has a singular focus on productivity as measured by prolificness, not depth or breadth. The energy to produce the one sensational gift takes a toll—and that's without knowing how many failures or mistakes informed the final result. The corpse flower doesn't grow to 12 feet in one year—it battles natural disasters and pests and diseases, at least in its natural habitat, to get to the point where it produces its iconic towering flower.

The daylily (*Hemerocallis)* got its common name quite literally—its individual flowers last only a single day. While the corpse flower rarely blooms, the daylily plant blooms each year and will often continue to flower for weeks, yet its individual flowers fade and drop before we may have a chance to appreciate each of them. Like a powerful speech, a moment of inspiring leadership, or a short-term project that creates change, the daylily focuses all its energy into a strong, bright flower for a limited time and plays to a limited audience. Like the stories we hear of heroism of the everyday person or perhaps someone at work that curates a workshop that offers lessons that improve our processes, these moments of brilliance may not extend as far as a work of classic literature or a one-hit wonder to which we know all the lyrics, but it is a singular achievement that has an impact which might extend farther than we'll ever know.

A TEDx Talk lasts 18 minutes. Many of these speakers may never appear on a world stage again, yet theoretically, their presentation will live on forever—just a Google topic search away from finding its next viewer for whom it could shift thinking and create a life change. Like the pollen from a daylily that may nourish a pollinator or become the honey that we use in our tea, that 18-minute TEDx Talk, perhaps less time than it takes to commute to work, continues to have an impact.

The unwritten rule that success is measured by quantity surely extends to our own self-judgment. While we don't judge the corpse flower for its one spectacular accomplishment, when we produce in ways that aren't considered the standard for our gender, family expectation, or any other social script that whispers in our brain, we start questioning our worth.

Humans are often critical of any situation in their lives that might deviate from an imaginary success measurement. But when we think about bloomtime, we also need to remember that the effects of our flowering don't end when our blooms fade. For example, a teacher has a career with a concentrated bloomtime—the school year. But the impact of a teacher doesn't end there. It can be felt for months, years, or even into the next generation.

Often, we know that our gifts to the world are the best part of us. But still, that social script and others' outside judgments bounce around inside our heads. Conversely, some people's gifts may appear more prolific. According to Guinness World Records, Agatha Christie is the most widely published author of all time in any language, having sold over two billion copies of her books. That is a distinct type of achievement—remarkable in its own way, yet different from one book that is taught and discussed in thousands of high school classrooms.

Similarly, in my garden, my catmint (*Nepeta*) blooms continually through the spring and summer year after year. Not only does it provide a reliable pop of color to my summer garden, but it is often covered with bees, flies, and butterflies; it's an important food source for many common pollinators. It chugs along, much like my coneflower, reliably and with little fuss. Both catmint and coneflower are frequently part of a sun garden design, due to their predictability and toughness.

Although we can take such a consistent performer for granted—these plants aren't likely to draw the crowds of the corpse flower—we would surely notice if they stopped performing. In much the same way, there are those humans whose impact is deeply felt, but not always seen. Reliable workers such as trash collectors or delivery drivers, as well as support staff, helpers, and listeners are prime examples of this. They are a part of our life landscape but are rarely offered the recognition and appreciation they deserve for their important contributions to our human ecosystem. Often, there are shining, lovely gifts in both plants and people that are not recognized—at least while the blooming is happening.

Then there is the diminutive lily of the valley (*Convallaria*). Like introverts, they grow in the coolness of shade while, like extroverts, they amass in colonies. (Does that make lily of the valley ambiverts?) Their leaves are upright, deep green blades and their flowers are dainty, often in shades of white or blush. They grow to barely six inches, yet their scent is sweet and unmistakable. Lily of the valley are tougher than they look, spreading when they are happy with their environment, but sticking to the shade, not extending past their comfort zone.

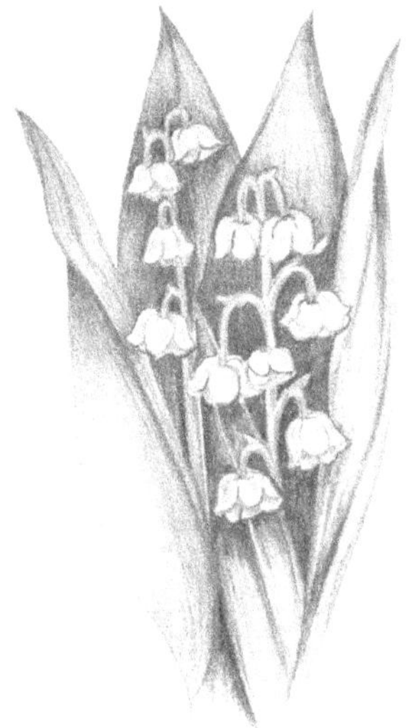

Lily of the valley (Convallaria)

One of my favorite plants, native to my state of Pennsylvania, is the mayapple (*Podophyllum*). One day a friend showed me the tiny white flower—fully hidden by the large, umbrella-shaped leaves—which would ultimately become a tiny, green, apple-shaped seed. The source of future mayapples is invisible unless you know where to look.

When I think about hidden gifts, I think about students who weren't successful by typical academic measures. The most well-known names in tech development of the early personal computer days, including Steve Jobs, Bill Gates, and Michael Dell, all who dropped out of college to pursue their ideas. I'm guessing there were plenty of nay-sayers when they made that decision, yet they grew to the point that their seeds have been strewn all over the world.

Mayapple (Podophyllum)

People on the neurodivergent spectrum are another example of those whose gifts may be overlooked due to the fact that their ways of thinking and acting fall outside traditional norms. One of the best examples is Temple Grandin, an autism advocate and pioneer in the world of humane livestock handling. She earned her PhD in a male-dominated field, and, through her ability to "think in pictures," she could envision solutions others could not. Her path to success was far from easy, and had she allowed the world to convince her that her hidden gifts were invalid or unimportant, she would not have achieved nearly as much as she did.

In the same way that we overlook the gifts of plants or people we misjudge, we tend to believe that challenging or inhospitable environments can't produce beauty. Yet there are flowers that bloom in situations that seem impossible, like the pringle manzanita (*Arctostaphylos pringlei*). This desert plant, growing on dry, rocky mountain slopes at an elevation of 4000–7500 feet, is found in the western United States. It produces clusters of tiny pink, bell-like flowers that eventually produce berries that feed birds, bears, and other animals. This incredible plant, hardy to extreme conditions that would threaten survival for many other plants or animals, including humans, would not survive in conditions with ample moisture and shade. Yet where it does thrive, it is a valuable source of food within the ecosystem.

Think about how this relates to careers that are extreme, such as war zone reporters, firefighters, or high-altitude or water rescuers. These people thrive in situations that would be untenable for the vast majority of us, yet their contributions provide valuable information and save lives. Even the average person can have times when they survive extreme conditions to nourish others. For example, when a loved one has a terminal diagnosis or we have a child with intense special needs, we are certainly inhabiting an emotional climate that pushes us to our limits, one that demands resilience. During challenging life situations, we find ways to create an environment where we can survive conditions we may not have ever imagined but through which we provide an essential role in the ecosystem.

Some of my favorite flowers are spring ephemerals. Although "ephemeral" may make these plants sound delicate, they are anything but. They are some of the earliest blooming native plants, coming into their full glory before the leaf canopy of the trees fills in. They both dazzle in the landscape and provide one of the earliest essential food sources for spring-emerging pollinators. Then they literally disappear (hence the "ephemeral" part).

Spring beauty (*Claytonia virginica*) and Virginia bluebells (*Mertensia virginica*) are two of my favorite spring ephemerals. While the color of a sunlit patch of Virginia bluebells is like the sky fell to earth, spring beauties are demure gems that have dashes of cotton candy pink on tiny white petals. And while these lovelies are filling an important function in the ecosystem, the example of their fleeting gifts shouldn't be undersold. Something as simple as an unexpected email, someone offering a simple act of grace, or a good Samaritan paying for your morning coffee can change the trajectory of your day. Any experience that leaves an impact, no matter how short, is a spring ephemeral.

Virginia bluebells (Mertensia virginica)

Everyone has gifts. They are all valuable. The smallest pebble dropped into a pond makes a ripple, and even the tiniest wildflower along the road will support a pollinator or be noticed by the kid in the backseat of the car. Bloom how you bloom. All the flowers are beautiful and important to their ecosystem.

And that may be the most important truth about gifts—while they enrich the world, they never exist in isolation. Each flower attracts its own pollinators, and while we often focus on what the bloom gives, it could not exist without that relationship. The very insects and animals that benefit from the flower also make its blooming possible.

The legacy we leave reflects both our lived experiences and the relationships that shaped us, while also serving as a catalyst for the gifts of others. Recognizing our importance within the community around us reminds us that our presence—seen or unseen—creates conditions for growth that may continue long after we are gone. We are both the flower and the pollinator.

Before we explore our pollinating relationships, consider how the aspects of your unique flowering relate to your Essential Nature, and how you both benefit your ecosystem and flourish.

Key Takeaways — Harvest the Fruit:

- **Everyone blooms differently—and every form of blooming matters.** Just as plants flower in different seasons, shapes, durations, and intensities, humans offer their gifts in unique ways. There is no single right pattern for impact.

- **Our culture often equates worth with consistency and prolific output**, yet nature reminds us that some of the most meaningful contributions are rare, brief, or deeply focused.

- **When environments are stressful or inhospitable, plants conserve energy** by limiting flowering. Humans do the same—and that is wisdom, not failure.

- **A single contribution can change an ecosystem.** One book, one invention, one moment of leadership, one conversation, one season of care can ripple outward far beyond what we ever see.

- **Hidden gifts are often overlooked in certain societies.** Neurodivergent minds, quiet contributors, reliable helpers, and those whose work happens behind the scenes are essential to the health of the whole ecosystem—even if they rarely receive recognition.

- **Your impact doesn't end when your visible blooming does.** The effects of your gifts often continue long after the moment has passed, carried forward in ways you may never witness.

Reflection Questions — Plant New Seeds:

- What patterns do you notice in how you've bloomed over time— and where have you compared your way of blooming to someone else's?

- Where in your life are you being asked to conserve energy or bloom more quietly, and how might restraint be wisdom rather than failure in this season?

- Looking back, what moments—small or visible—have created lasting impact, and what does that tell you about your gifts and the value of blooming authentically?

CHAPTER 5 POLLINATION:

What is your legacy?

"Collaboration is the essence of life. The wind, bees, and flowers work together to spread the pollen."

— Amit Ray

"Every person has a legacy. You may not know what your impact is, and it may not be something that you can write on your tombstone, but every person has an impact on this world."

— Dara Horn

Pollination is fertilization, also known as plant sexual reproduction. Plants have sex cells just as humans do: Sperm cells are carried within the pollen grains, which are produced in the anther. This is part of the stamen, the male reproductive structure of a flower. Bees, for example, gather pollen on their legs as they move from flower to flower. In doing so, they deposit pollen (sperm) from one flower onto another. The pistil, or central part of most flowers, is the female reproductive structure, which consists of three parts. The pollen lands on the topmost part, called the stigma, and it travels down the tubelike structure of the style. This is similar to sperm traveling through human fallopian tubes. The pollen then ends up in the bottom part of the pistil, which is called, appropriately, the ovary, where it can fertilize the egg. The result of a successful pollination is a seed, the equivalent of a human zygote or the initial fusion of a human sperm and egg.

Reproductive parts of a flower

While pollen literally encompasses half the genetic material to create new life for the plant, it is also the sustaining nourishment of many pollinators, including bees, flies, wasps, and beetles. For bees, especially, pollen is a crucial food source. They feed their larvae (baby bees) as well as themselves from this rich source of essential nutrients. It is vital to their survival. The flower's nectar is the enticement for the process of secondary pollination. When butterflies visit to feed on nectar, pollen granules stick to their bodies. The process of fertilization is completed as the butterflies flit from flower to flower, gathering and depositing pollen in their search for nourishment. Flowering is the plant's way of not only continuing its own legacy but of nourishing its ecosystem in an amazing symbiotic relationship with pollinators.

Humans have our own ways of attracting what we need to procreate—and of course this term means much more than creating offspring. Erick Erikson, a 20th century psychologist known for his theory of human development, devoted an entire stage of life to *generativity*—what legacy do we leave in the world? For some people, it can be inspirational writing, a structure of amazing architecture, or an Oscar-winning movie. But some of the most impactful legacies are less lofty but no less important: teaching or parenting children, imparting knowledge or providing mentorship.

These are really our gifts—the flowers—that we explored in the previous chapter.

But we all have people and situations that contribute to the pollination that allows us to grow and share our gifts. Who "pollinates" us? What beautiful experience or terrible tragedy planted the seeds for the gifts that *you* produce and share with the world?

We sometimes make the mistake of believing that the path to success is straight and smooth, but it's often the harshest environments that produce the hardiest plants. Just like winds make saplings into sturdier trees with more secure roots, a smooth, easy road isn't the typical path traversed by artists and sages. We learn from mistakes, challenges, and losses. Navigating the tough times is how we understand how to grow into the best version of ourselves.

For many, this journey begins with their parents. When I was a kid, I thought my parents were perfect. Later in life, with the help of maturity and therapy, the cracks in their "perfection" became much more apparent. Either way, I know they both loved me in the best way they knew how. And now the way they loved me is woven into every aspect of my life: the sacrifices to pay for college with one income and five children (an advantage I never knew other kids didn't automatically have), a clean home with consistent care and concern, a much-loved pet, and always having laughter, even if it was sometimes scattered by outside stressors, like the violence of an addicted sibling.

I chose to tattoo the word "love" on my arm twice—one in each parent's handwriting—to remind myself that I'm a product of how they expressed it. This helps me be mindful in spreading the best of that and tempering the worst. I take the effects of their love with me through all my days.

When I think of my own parents' consistency, I often think of the converse: inconsistent, cruel, or absent parents. Whether I was working with elementary, high school, or college students, it was a rare week when I didn't see the effects of being raised by these types of parents on my young clients. The impact of that parenting varied widely from student to student, as their own Essential Nature tempered the effects.

Abuse is what we imagine creates the most indelible impact on children and their futures. It's a little known fact that the vast majority of abused children do not, themselves, grow up to be abusers, yet it always has an impact on their future relationships and ways of interacting with the world. And amazingly, sometimes the most cruelly abused children show the most resilience. However, they need to find adaptations to survive, just like plants that are in inhospitable environments. In fact, individual plants of the same species can adapt quite differently to similar environmental impacts.

For example, last year I noticed that the leaves of my lenten roses (*Helleborus*) were covered with dozens of white specks. Aphids! (Otherwise known as small insects that feed on plant sap and often damage plant growth.) The pests got a good headstart before I noticed them. I sprayed the leaves with my hose nozzle set to "jet" and cut off the leaves with the worst infestations. Then I hoped for the best.

Of the three plants with infestations, each recovered at a different rate— one, in particular, seemed to take longer to regrow normal leaves. However, by the time the plants flowered the following March, they all seemed back to their full form.

Why did the impact of the damage vary on each of the plants? One explanation could be that I had planted three different varieties. In midsummer, without their flowers, they all looked the same, even to the trained eye. But for some reason, one plant out of the three struggled to bounce back. Perhaps it received a different amount of sunlight or the least amount of rainfall due to being closer to the house. Even in the plant world, it can be difficult to tease apart the impact of genetics and environment.

The same is true with people. The impact of a rough home environment can be mitigated by other factors in the environment; this is why mental health programs from early childhood through high school are vitally important. But one issue we don't often consider is the impact of *epigenetics* on how we navigate our world.

Epigenetics considers how environment and behavior affect how our genes function. The impacts on genes can include diet, stress, toxins, and experiences. While these do not cause actual changes in our physical DNA, epigenetic markers influence the expression of our genes. For example, imagine your entire DNA code like a textbook—and someone has used a highlighter on it. It's like telling your body which parts to read and which parts to skip *without changing the actual words.* And the most astounding aspect of these epigenetic marks is that trauma from one generation can be expressed in the next generation.

Let's consider how epigenetics affects plants. Because nature's goal is survival and procreation, plants will "remember" certain environmental stressors by marking its DNA. For example, we know that plants adapt to conditions that aren't optimal by adjusting the color or surface area of their leaves to either increase their ability to gather the sun's energy or limit their photosynthesizing, depending on their preferred conditions. And, if you remember, some plants can also produce their own sunscreen in the form of flavonoids. Thale cress (*Arabidopsis thaliana*) uses this protective response and, after activating flavonoids, codes its genes so that this reaction will occur more quickly in the future. Further, the genes of the plant's offspring will often carry this adaptation forward, increasing their ability to respond to threats more efficiently.

You might be thinking, "This is interesting, but how does it relate to pollination and legacy and all that?" Hang with me for one more example.

We've explored the wide range of climates and even nutritional assets of the dandelion. Although maligned by some as a lowly weed, it's pretty amazing in its ability to adapt, as well as in its usefulness as a healthy food. So it's no surprise that it can serve as an example of the range of epigenetic modification: Two plants from the same parent can adjust to vastly different growing conditions—one can adapt to tolerate drought, while the other can accelerate its growth rate in rich soil. Each plant has the same textbook, but different sections are highlighted!

Now I can bring this back around: I began this chapter with the mechanics of pollination—plant sexual reproduction. But here's the key: This process depends on pollinators. They aren't just moving pollen; they're facilitating genetic diversity, strengthening ecosystems, and ensuring the health of future growth.

We, too, act as "pollinators" in our human environments. The way we show up, connect, and support one another has ripple effects that nurture resilience, diversity, and balance within our communities. Something as simple as serving as a mentor—or seeking out your own sources of encouragement—creates lasting change. Like the steady work of bees or butterflies, our consistent presence can help others thrive, while also bringing more vitality and strength to the whole ecosystem we share. While it may be easy to underestimate our own influence in the face of someone else's trauma, we don't need to start a nonprofit or find a cure for cancer to have an important impact. We can think of it in degrees: Even small efforts are part of a scaffold of positive support for a human ecosystem.

Plants assist pollinators in a crucial way beyond producing nectar. *Host plants* are specific species whose foliage serves as the food sources for the larval stage (caterpillar) of butterflies and moths. And while some insects are generalists—their larvae can feed on a variety of plants—others co-evolved to need a specific plant to feed their young. One example is my beloved violet (*Viola*), the host plant of the Great Spangled Fritillary. This dainty-looking, yet scrappy beauty tends to live under the radar, spreading readily through my lawn and into my flower beds, where it is welcome. Likewise, milkweed (*Asclepias),* the host plant of the monarch butterfly, has leaves that produce sticky, thick juices that cannot sustain the larvae of other butterfly species. But unlike prolific violets, milkweed is disappearing. This is alarming on many levels.

Common violet (Viola)

While most butterflies live out their life cycle in a relatively small area, monarchs migrate south to Mexico for the winter. After overwintering in the warmer climate, they begin their flight north in March. As they migrate, they stop their journey to lay their eggs. This is the next generation: When those eggs hatch and the caterpillars morph into adult butterflies, they continue the flight north. By August, the cycle is complete, and the fourth generation of monarchs begin their flight south, sometimes laying the eggs of the next generation on their journey.

Knowing that the only plant species that can support monarch larvae is milkweed, what does that mean for each generation? There need to be consistent sources of it in the landscape along their journey. Each plant matters.

When you think about what sustains you and how you leave a legacy for the future, perhaps you can think of mentors or important adults from your life that were there to give you what you needed at a key moment. Or when you think of your impact, you can recognize that you don't need to do it all—you just need to be part of the overall ecosystem that supports individuals. Even if you intersect with someone only for a season, you are giving them part of what they desire—or getting some of what you desire—to create a thriving future.

Perhaps you can think of a time when you required a deeper connection or a higher level of care. Or maybe you offered that to someone else. If a friend has a crisis or experiences a loss, a relationship that may have historically been based on shared interests or fun activities can shift and require a more intentional presence. If you are the one that tends to offer this, either as a function of your career or your role in your relationships, you are giving a unique gift to your environment. If you've ever experienced this—someone noticing a potential in you that others may have overlooked, for example—it can be a gift you pass on.

As a school counselor, I was given ample opportunities to "pollinate" and leave my legacy—sometimes without recognizing the extent of the impact. One year, in the first month of school, there was a tragedy, a freak accident that ended in the death of one boy. His friends, including his girlfriend, had to navigate their senior year in the wake of this devastating loss. I met with all of them, as a group and individually, over the course of that year. I rode with them through the myriad of emotions as they coped with grief and guilt in their own ways.

At the end of that school year, each graduate was required to fill out a senior survey to gather data on their paths after high school: college, military, the workforce, etc. In the comments, the girlfriend of the boy who died expressed gratitude for the support she and her friends received from school staff that year. Then she wrote that I had saved her life.

Sometimes that's how pollination works. I was just doing my job and taking actions that anyone in my position would. It was my ecosystem; I was one of the pollinators who evolved to do the exact work of helping the next generation of young people to grow. In this case, the system was in crisis, so my ability to help them adapt and write resilience into their genes quite literally saved a life.

Sometimes pollination gives future gifts a chance to grow simply through a "right time, right place" serendipity that creates ripples of change—that time when one choice, maybe to gamble instead of playing it safe, creates a spark that ignites many future choices.

Remember my new boss who completely changed the climate of my work environment, leaving me ragged and in survival mode? When I finally left that job, I felt adrift—lost and unsure where I would belong.

But now I am grateful. Because it was my Essential Nature—my inability to tolerate unfair treatment of myself or any of my colleagues—that spurred my decision to leave a job I loved. As the jewelweed only knows how to leave its legacy by an explosion of seed, I knew that the parts of my Thrivability Zone had changed so much that I would never be able to share my gifts or be the pollinator for others that I had been my entire career. The improbable constellation of events leading to my resignation gave me the opportunity to grow to a new height and have more unique blooms than I ever imagined. I believe there was a significant dollop of serendipity to it all. Only now can I see it was truly a case of right time, right place, allowing me to step more fully into my Essential Nature.

For fruit bats and the baobab tree (*Adansonia digitata*), right time, right place is crucial. The tree blooms under cover of darkness, with flowers measuring five to eight inches across and hanging down on stalks that can reach nearly three feet in length. The flowers open and close, sometimes within 15 hours, once every six months. Therefore, the baobab tree needs specific pollinators to work quickly during the night. Fruit bats do the work, and this, in turn, produces fruits that can last without preservatives for three years. Although the bats need to be ready to pollinate during a brief window, their work brings a measured investment that pays out over the longterm. It is what is needed by the plant and in that system—swift but crucial impact, long-term dividend.

Does one seemingly insignificant interaction impact your mood for the rest of the day? It can be a smile; it can be someone darting into a parking space ahead of you. Remember that you can grow whatever flower you want from that interaction. Not every relationship is mutually beneficial. Sometimes responding to a parasite—someone taking energy and not offering anything positive—with acceptance is better for your health and the wellbeing of the ecosystem. The fruit bat gets paid in nectar when it pollinates the baobab tree, but surely the tree is getting the better end of the bargain at no expense to the pollinator.

If you are that person who takes an extra second from your day to connect, who sends a text when you think of someone, or takes an extra minute to talk to the server in a restaurant, you may be creating a shift in the ecosystem that goes farther than you'll ever know.

We've explored so much about the interdependence of pollinators and plants in nature that you may be surprised to know that there are flowers that are *self-pollinating*.

Plants that self-pollinate have both male and female reproductive parts and can be fertilized by their own pollen. At times this can happen before the flowers are fully open, which also negates the need for help from pollinators, like insects or the wind. Plants that can self-pollinate are varied. The most common are wheat, rice, barley, and oats. Other plants also self-pollinate, but typically still need some help from other pollinators. For example, the strong vibration of bumblebees often facilitates self-pollination of tomatoes. The bee isn't physically transferring pollen with its body but instead, with the collateral impact of its buzzing.

So you may be wondering, why don't all plants have the ability to self-pollinate? Wouldn't that make life easier?

One important factor limiting the future legacy of self-pollinating plants is that it can reduce genetic diversity. If an offspring develops weaker traits from the parent plant, that trait will continue to be expressed and could impact the survival of the species, at least in that colony of plants. Or, as we've seen with epigenetics, any adaptation that increases resilience cannot be shared with other plants in the species, potentially limiting the number of plants in the next generation that have adapted to overcome environmental challenges.

As we've seen, plants that coevolve with specific pollinators can enjoy the benefits of that symbiosis … when conditions are optimal. What happens when there is an environmental impact that influences the health and availability of those pollinators? How will the plants that cannot be fertilized by their own pollen actually procreate without outside help? Balancing our ability, as humans, to self-pollinate (being autonomous and self-reliant) with appropriately accepting and receiving help from others puts us closer to the apex of thriving. We can evolve intentionally to be more independent in our pollination and to strategically work within our environment to grow and support our legacy and, in turn, do the same for others.

Having the ability to accept cross-pollination is a key survival aspect, ensuring survival of the most adaptable traits. In the case of humans and how we are pollinated by our environment, the more able we are to reach beyond our own resources when needed, the better our own ability becomes to adapt to life changes, especially crises. Just as an extreme season or a natural disaster can impact the ability of our coevolved pollinators to be available, life events can impact how people in our support network are able to show up or how situations, like the end of a job, can impact financial security.

Being self-pollinating is a wonderful ability and a needed adaptation for us all, but recognize that, even in flowers that have everything they need to leave a legacy, outside forces help them accomplish it. Nature is a community, an interrelated system. What we do either adds to or negatively impacts our ecosystem. From the smallest action to the boldest one, we are constantly giving and receiving. We are highlighting the passages of our DNA textbook that we will continue to read. Building your self-pollination ability, while expanding the supports in your ecosystem to increase your versatility and viability for thriving, will leave a legacy with far-reaching impacts.

Even the most prolific pollinators have a cycle of rest that is informed by their nature. And they build their relationships and achievements in ways that honor that. While bees and butterflies pollinate during the day, moths are nocturnal, fertilizing and feeding from plants whose blooms open when other pollinators are taking a nightly respite. Without these varying rest cycles, the needs of the ecosystem couldn't be met. And without rest, pollinators couldn't survive to do their work.

Take some time to reflect on your pollinating strengths and strategies. Next we'll consider how this is woven into our own unique needs for daily and seasonal rest.

Key Takeaways — Harvest the Fruit:

- **Pollination is about legacy, not just reproduction.** In nature, pollination ensures genetic diversity and future vitality. In human terms, it mirrors generativity—the ways we create meaning, influence others, and leave something behind through our gifts, relationships, and care for future generations.

- **Our gifts don't develop in isolation**—they are shaped by what "pollinates" us. People, experiences, losses, mentors, and even hardships all act as pollinators, planting the seeds that shape what we eventually offer the world.

- **Difficult conditions often produce the most resilient growth.** Just as wind strengthens trees and harsh environments create hardy plants, human resilience and wisdom are often forged through struggle, not ease.

- **Genetics, environment, Essential Nature, and epigenetics all influence how people adapt to adversity.** Two people can experience similar conditions and emerge with very different outcomes.

- **We are both pollinators and hosts within our ecosystems.** Our presence—whether as mentors, listeners, caregivers, colleagues, or quiet supporters—can profoundly shape others' ability to thrive, even when we don't recognize the impact in the moment.

- **Small, consistent acts often matter more than grand gestures.** Legacy is rarely built only through monumental achievements. Often it's created through everyday connection, timing, and presence—the human equivalent of bees quietly doing essential work.

- **Thriving requires both self-sufficiency and openness to help.** Like self-pollinating plants, humans benefit from independence, but long-term vitality depends on connection, diversity, and the willingness to receive support when needed.

Reflection Questions — Plant New Seeds:

- How do you define legacy for yourself—large or small, visible or quiet—and where are you already living that impact in everyday ways?

- Which experiences—especially the hard or uncertain ones—shaped the strengths and gifts you carry now, and what do they reveal about your Essential Nature and capacity for compassion?

- Where do you offer pollination to others, and how can you also allow yourself to receive support and sustenance without explanation or self-justification?

CHAPTER 6 DORMANCY AND VERNALIZATION:

How do you rest and find peace?

"The madness of spring is so enticing. I love it when things are opening up and emerging from the ground. I also love the middle of summer when fruit is bursting forth, but I even love the garden in the winter when everything is resting."

— Ross Gay

"Winter reminds me that even nature needs time to rest and return to its roots."

— Unknown

All beings have cycles of rest, including plants. The type of rest needed for plants can vary widely based on their needs and their unique growth. Similar to hibernation for animals, *dormancy* is when plants slow or stop their growth. Unlike hibernation, dormancy is not based solely on the cycle of seasons. It is brought on by any condition not conducive to helping the plant grow. This includes temperature extremes or a shortage in nutrients, as well as conditions that are too wet or too dry.

Aside from responses to extreme conditions, plants have characteristic daily cycles of rest. It is common for flowers to close their petals at night. One example that comes to mind is the common violet (*Viola sororia*). In fact, the tendency for violets to close their petals at night resulted in a common misconception that they were too dainty or fragile. This led to the "shrinking violet" term used in Victorian times to describe women who were quiet or demure. This was a gross underestimation of the violet (and, to be honest, women), as violets, while appearing delicate, are some of the hardiest and most useful plants found in my geographic area. They simply fold themselves closed at night to conserve energy and, practically, their pollinators aren't active at night.

If a plant doesn't have what it needs—or if it's overwhelmed by too much—it naturally pulls back. Humans are no different. We, too, need the right conditions to flourish, and those conditions look a little different for each of us.

The daily dormancy pattern for humans is sleep. The entire natural world is calibrated to support rest, even in humans. However, in our modern world of light pollution, screens, and 24/7 forms of distraction, it can be difficult to remember that there was a time when the only light we had was the sun. Or a full moon. Our bodies were designed to equate darkness with sleep. This cycle is called *circadian rhythm*. Melatonin, the hormone that relaxes us and prepares our minds and bodies for sleep, starts increasing late in the day and peaks after dark. Cortisol, a hormone that increases alertness and prepares our mind and body to energize for the day, starts increasing as the sun rises.

Just like plants—and all of nature—we are designed to sleep, although we often think it's negotiable and that we can "indulge" in sleep when it's convenient to our schedules.

Nothing is farther from the truth. The impact of poor sleep touches every part of our lives. Deep sleep begins soon after we fall asleep and, during this stage, cerebrospinal fluid moves through the brain, helping clear out toxins and restore it. The REM (Rapid Eye Movement) stage—our dreaming stage—helps consolidate memory. Sleep disruptions upend nearly all of our hormones. Hormones, the chemical messengers for all the processes of our bodies, function as an orchestra: Any change in one can result in a change in others. Even *ghrelin* and *leptin*, hormones that regulate appetite, are disrupted by poor sleep, which can result in weight gain. If sleep is dysregulated long enough, it can lend to a cascade of health issues, from anxiety and depression to heart disease and Alzheimer's.

If you struggle with sleep issues, it could be a result of a disrupted hormonal pattern impacting the availability of melatonin or an excess of cortisol at night. Often, daytime stresses exert their influence at night, resulting in restless sleep, frequent waking, or even anxiety. If we were plants, we would recognize the dysregulation and instinctively rely on nature's cue to establish homeostasis and restore our sleep cycle. However, humans tend to lead with our thinking brains and mentally minimize the impact of insufficient sleep; we don't recognize how crucial it is for our health and thriving. In fact, we have normalized the Western "hustle culture" and the resulting hormone dysregulation and sleep deprivation. Although we now have medical means that can ameliorate health issues caused in part by poor rest, reconnecting to nature's light and dark cycle is a starting point to stave off sleep deprivation health issues before they start.

Beyond our daily need for sleep, what about our daily energy optimization? In many ways, the ideal habits for plant health mirror the best habits for human health. Watering plants first thing in the morning or after sundown allows the water to be absorbed by the roots before the sun of the day can create stress. Additionally, plants respond to conditions during the day by instinctively conserving resources. If a plant receives too much sun—or the sun is simply too intense—it often wilts, as explained in chapter 2. This is a way to conserve energy.

Being both intentional with our wellness practices (staying hydrated) and being responsive to our changing energy (taking a nap or a walk) helps us stay present and engaged. Planning activities at the times of day that are optimal for our own nature helps us be productive. For example, I do my most thought-intensive work mid-morning when my brain naturally feels alert.

Often, however, we allow outside agendas to dictate how we manage our energy. This is important sometimes, such as working on a deadline or when we need to care for an ill child. But when we struggle to keep up with these responsibilities or we aren't functioning at the top of our game, we tend to believe that we just need to "try harder."

Putting aside perceived limits and reflecting on the needs of your Essential Nature can be a starting point in truly understanding how you function best. Remember that plants instinctively do what they must to meet their needs. We are nature too. Plus we have much more autonomy. If you could design your workday the way you'd like, incorporating your priorities, what would it look like? When does your energy ebb and flow? Where are you making choices that ultimately make you feel worse or exacerbate the mismatches in your own needs versus the imposed agenda?

Start with what you need: a healthy lunch? Time to move during the day? Or time for mindfulness or a short meditation? Now work backward. What do you need to make those things happen? Sometimes the first step is to prioritize making lunches on the weekend so you can grab something healthy each day. Sometimes it means taking charge of the aspects of your schedule that you do have control over.

Because I worked for most of my career in environments that could be unpredictable and that required the ability to respond to crises as part of the service model, managing the aspects of my daily agenda that I *did* have control over was important. First, I scheduled periodic respites so I could show up fully for each client. Part of this strategy was blocking off a lunch hour every day using the "repeat daily" feature on my electronic calendar. This was an easy, proactive way to protect my time—I could always move or change it later, if needed. And while I know some therapists who schedule appointments back-to-back, leaving little time for notes or even a bathroom break, that wasn't sustainable for me. I scheduled two clients, maximum, back to back, with a break after that to complete the notes for those appointments. Ultimately, this allowed me to complete my tasks and end my day at a reasonable time, even accounting for one or two unexpected issues—without feeling exhausted and depleted.

Working in a way that doesn't optimize our energy not only compromises our wellbeing, but it also means that we cannot bring our most effective self to our work. Remember that having specific preferences does not mean you're not achieving (no matter what management tells you); it means that you have an Essential Nature, and can no more have maximal production with a compromised environment than a tulip could bloom all summer.

We all have seasonal energy fluctuations. We can assume they are matched to our cultural seasons—summer vacations or holidays, for example. But our own inner compass might be pointing south when we assume it needs to point north. When I hear people talk about their favorite seasons, the least likely one people choose is winter—at least here in the middle northeast United States. Think about it for a minute: What is truly your most comfortable season? The one in which you feel most alive, most motivated? Winter is the quintessential time of rest and renewal, both in nature and in mythology.

Even in ancient times, humans recognized that there was a cycle to the seasons, although the Greeks equated winter with sorrow and summer with joy. But even today, winter is often equated with a lower energy, a time of reckoning. And spring is equated with awakening, new energy, and unfurling.

What are plants doing during the typical winter months? In areas where we experience winters of cold and ice or snow, water is often shifted out of the cells and into the roots, making the plant less susceptible to freezing. Deciduous, broadleaf trees, like maples *(Acer)* and oaks *(Quercus),* shed their leaves to drastically reduce water loss from the collective surface area of all those leaves. But why do they change color?

Remember that chlorophyll, the green in leaves, facilitates photosynthesis, or energy production. Because the tree is downshifting to protect itself and prepare for rest, it stops producing chlorophyll. This may allow other colors of the leaves to assert themselves, once the green color is absent, but more amazing is that the tree absorbs the nutrients from the leaves to fortify itself for its winter rest.

If you've ever driven through the upper east coast of the United States in the fall, the colors are stunning. My late mother-in-law called these trips "leaf peeping," but I always thought that seemed too tame. The sweep of fiery displays cover the surrounding hills. The process would seem startling to us, if we had never experienced it. We would think it was surely a disease or an anomaly, because in what world does such a dramatic transformation occur without a permanent outcome? Yet, come spring, the leaves bud and open as if nothing happened.

But that dormancy is crucial for their survival. You know what happens to a pipe full of water in freezing temperatures? It expands and breaks because frozen water expands. The fate of tree cells could be similar, if they didn't go through a dormancy period and protect themselves.

Trees are genetically programmed to begin dormancy based on environmental cues—namely, diminishing light and colder temperatures. As the days get shorter and the sun's arc is lower in the sky, photosynthesis is impacted. So for us, reflecting on the cues in our own environment is key to our awareness of when we need to downshift.

As we talked about with our Thrivability Zone, recognizing the aspects of our environment that allow us to find this seasonal dormancy cycle connected to our Essential Nature is an important factor. Are there aspects of your environment that you are allowing to impact you in a negative way? Do you set high expectations for holidays or family events or even work projects? Recognizing the cycle of dormancy that helps your body naturally thrive can be much more impactful to your success than pushing yourself to achieve a contrived or imposed goal. And sometimes this dormancy may just be an inner loosening or letting go of expectations as a means to reset our own goals and expectations.

However, not all trees take such a dramatic break. Some trees and perennials are evergreen; they are typically more impervious to moisture loss during cold weather. One of my favorites is holly (*Ilex*), of which there are many varieties. Through winter, they can have green or variegated leaves and bright, red berries, an important food source for birds and other wildlife. Holly leaves are waxy and tough, which provides protection from the cold. As holly flowers in early spring, it may appear that it doesn't rest—it is not the visible powering down that we can appreciate in deciduous trees, which drop their leaves in autumn and bud out again in spring. Instead, the holly bush focuses on root development and saves new growth for spring. Although it looks vibrant and alive in a way that deciduous trees may not, it has simply done its work, produced its berries, and taken a silent, internal break.

It can be easy to assume that other people don't have their own rest cycle because they appear to be consistently vibrant. But like the holly, whose sharp, green leaves and bright red berries shine in the winter landscape, their appearance doesn't tell the whole story. They started their work to produce those berries months before winter, and now, when their work is done and the berries feed the ecosystem, they begin the hidden process of adding strength to their foundation—their roots—in preparation for the next cycle of flowers in the spring.

Trees "plan ahead" too. They don't just decide at the beginning of autumn that they are going to stop producing chlorophyll, downshift their growth, or shed their leaves. They are preparing—it is a hormonal response. And what are the physiological messengers of *our* body's cycles and processes? Hormones. Our bodies literally function based on cycles—puberty, and for women specifically, their ovulatory cycle and, eventually, menopause. For everyone, sleep. These are cycles that naturally occur based on the orchestra of our hormones.

But what if you suddenly recognize that you need something different than your usual seasonal rhythm of rest? Let's say you are the organizer of a family holiday celebration. Maybe as the holiday organizer, your energy feeds off your love of the season or the excitement it creates for others. If you're truly managing your fuel based on what others expect, that's a recipe for burnout.

Even if you choose to be the organizer-in-chief, there may be life events that require increased energy or that cause you to need more frequent rest to recharge. For example, illness, loss, or a traumatic event all require temporary adjustments. When we experience situations that require us to adjust, the effect spans our emotional, physical, mental, and spiritual faculties. Most of us don't immediately recognize our exhaustion or our different metabolic needs because we are so used to our typical rhythm. But switching our energy output from external events to our internal reserves will eventually be inevitable, whether we recognize it and make a conscious choice or our overall health suffers.

Hyacinths (*Hyancinthus orientalus),* tulips, and daffodils are often sold in the United States during the spring holidays of Easter and Mother's Day. As these special occasions sometimes occur before my own garden bulbs flower, I am defenseless against the intoxicating scent of the hyacinths, in particular. There is often a rotation of freshly blooming flowers on my dining table, depending on my trips to the grocery store.

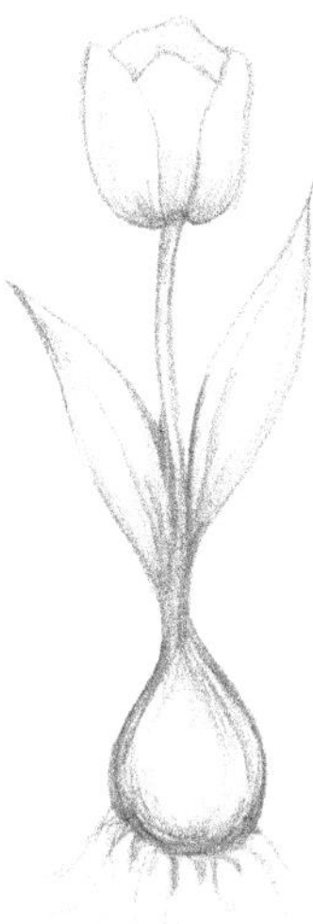

Tulip bulb

No surprise, these bulbs were grown in greenhouses and timed (read: forced) to bloom according to the schedule of human holidays. This means that the bulbs themselves were not able to vernalize according to the true needs of the plant. Although I frequently pop the bulbs into my garden beds after the flowers are spent, the resulting blooms the following spring are puny and weak, if they even make an appearance at all. This is a classic example of what happens to a plant that isn't afforded the opportunity to honor its Essential Nature and rest to recharge.

In the case of our tendency to de-priortize our own needs, it is nearly always fueled by the nagging of our inner critic. We postpone the inevitable (and worsen our mental or physical situation) because emotions come up when this gremlin perceives that we would deign to change our tactics to prioritize our rest. "Others are counting on this!" "I don't want to burden others." "I don't want to ruin the holiday for everyone."

What would plants do (WWPD)? A plant would instinctively recognize an energy drain and respond accordingly. Sometimes this means it shuts down, many examples of which we have already explored. At other times, it means they adapt to get more of what they need. Mangroves (*Rhizophora mangle*) are the poster children for surviving in rough or even inhospitable conditions that would kill other plants quickly. Mangroves are shrubby trees that grow in warm, tropical climates along coastlines and tidal rivers. The water where they thrive is salty and brackish, so they have adapted ways to take in extra oxygen, as well as survive the changing tides and remove salt from the water. They are protectors of their niche ecosystem.

Due to the high salt content of the water, the leaf structure of mangroves are engineered to limit the amount of water naturally lost from evaporation. Just as some plants develop adventitious roots, mangroves develop *prop roots* to raise themselves above the water level and absorb air through their bark. Some species even develop root structures like drinking straws that serve as "breathing tubes"—sometimes over three meters high!

Maybe you're thinking, *what could possibly happen that would create a crisis for the mangrove? It's so badass*! Well, the environmental conditions where it lives are already harsh. So it knows it needs to slow its growth when environmental ebbs and flows occur, like tidal changes or temporarily increases in salinity. But these are small potatoes compared to the challenge it faces from the habits of humans: climate change.

As we explored when we looked at climate zones and how plants try to adapt to changing conditions, mangroves are increasingly affected by rising sea levels, more intense storms, and more erratic rainfall patterns. When sea levels rise, coastal erosion can lead to mangrove forests shrinking or even disappearing. These are situations they are genetically programmed to adapt to as they occur, but the modern climate changes are drastic, even by mangrove standards. They have reached their limits of adaptation. Without human intervention to correct or mediate these impacts, we will continue to lose this unique and valuable champion of tidal ecosystems.

That may serve as a warning for those of us who are "doers," who always seem to rise to the needs of others or of the situation. We often have quite amazing adaptation abilities. Maybe we grow the equivalent of a temporary breathing tube to bring in support from other sources, or we alter our roots to bring in additional nutrients—food, emotional, or even financial support. But failing to adapt when conditions worsen means we create a crisis of larger proportions; we cannot maintain ourselves in the face of the onslaught. As vital components in nurturing and protecting our own human ecosystem, we must still recognize when we need to limit growth and focus on our own survival, even if it means we cannot do as much for those around us until our environment stabilizes.

Perhaps we are on the opposite end of the seasonal continuum from the mangrove. When other people travel for holidays or celebrate loudly, right in the middle of the melee, or they look forward to the reunion or other yearly blowout, we may, instead, decide to hunker down. Perhaps the thought of traveling during busy holiday seasons is the antithesis of a good time.

WWPD? The tamarack or American larch (*Larix laricina*) is a conifer that thrives in extremely cold zones, including central Alaska and as far northwest as the Yukon Territories. Its native growing conditions include boggy and poorly-drained soils. Unlike the majority of pine trees, tamaracks' needles turn golden, similarly to the leaves of deciduous trees, and fall to the ground as winter sets in.

American larch branch (Larix laricina)

What makes this needled tree behave differently than the majority of conifers? Its preferred growing conditions probably gave you a clue. Extreme conditions require different types of rest, and the tamarack has evolved to bridge the adaptive traits found in both conifers and deciduous trees. Even with its slim needles, it would continue to lose water through transpiration, and by shedding its needles, it reduces its surface area, making it easier to minimize water loss. It absorbs nitrogen from the needles and stores it for use until spring. The other advantage of reducing its surface area is that this will limit damage of broken branches from snow loads, thus making them more resilient. Finally, needle-less branches are less susceptible to fire and insect damage. Genius survival tricks for a challenging winter environment.

What if a tamarack had a human brain with the ability to compare itself to, say, a pine tree, which typically retains its needles and continues to photosynthesize in the winter? It might decide it needs to maintain its quintessential evergreen-ness and hold on to its needles. That would be to its own peril, as that's not how tamaracks were built. They have their own Essential Nature that helps them survive their unique environment.

Each of us were designed with unique ways of thriving in the seasonal fluctuations of life. As humans, we have more autonomy than plants do to change our environmental situation. We can strategically find a place of thriving that serves our own inner need to rest and restore ourselves. Tamaracks and mangroves are both amazing specimens of ecosystem heroes and shrewd adaptation. However, would we judge them the same way if they were human, and their ways of being seemed socially strange or even dramatic and irrational? Although it's often a meme or the line beneath an email signature, it's true that each of us is fighting a battle no one truly knows about. And each of us, fully standing in our own Essential Natures, are amazing too. Adjusting isn't weird, adapting isn't high maintenance, and rest is not lazy—they are extraordinary skills, specific to our environment and our changing situations.

When I first started my business, I frantically tried one thing after another—all the strategies that made other people successful. Well, none of those things—or, to be honest, those people—rang true. Their way didn't resonate with what I wanted to build. Yet it was hard to calm my mind and make myself step back and assess. Because if I took a rest and just listened to what felt aligned for me, it felt weird. Unsettled.

However, this is the space we need to inhabit in order to rest and simply figure out how to move forward with intention and alignment; this is *liminal space*. Such a lovely word. It means a state of in-betweenness, not fully in the old but not yet in the new. Plants do this like champions through their cycles of rest and even with their strategically-timed blooming to maximize their gifts to the world.

Yet how often do humans rest in this liminal space? Uncertainty can feel overwhelming. We like to know where we're headed, what to plan for, and how to get there. Yet, really, the only place we can truly be is in the moment. We can look back with regrets or forward with anxiety, but that only spoils the present. And the present is all there is.

The coffee plant (*Coffea arabica*) produces what many of us consider the nectar of mornings. Yet it won't be rushed. The fruit ripens slowly—it hangs out on the branch until it feels ready to give up its amazing gift. The plant knows it needs to manage the energy it's using so that it can fill those prized beans with human optimism in the form of caffeine.

And similar to the corpse flower, which seems to rest and pool its resources to create one amazing, odiferous bloom, the sago palm (*Cycas revoluta*) only puts out new growth every few years. Dating back 200 million years and native to Japan and southern China, the sago palm is not a true palm. Its leaves grow in spurts or flushes, with rests in between. Overall, it is a slow grower, often taking 50 years or longer to reach its full height. In the case of the sago palm, it is quite easy to grow as a houseplant. Its measured leaf production, with resting phases in between, seems to work to its advantage.

For both the coffee plant and the sago palm, existing periodically in a type of plant-y liminal space helps them produce either coveted fruit in the form of coffee beans or foster their own longevity.

When we grow with intentionality, whether it's in preparation of our next project or in creation of something that takes a longer investment, we benefit from the advantage of stillness, of conserving energy that may be wasted on haste. It may not always be obvious that shifts are happening out of sight, yet a mindful awareness of the present moment will yield a richer outcome. In the same way that impatience may cause a premature harvest of unripened coffee bean (thus, waste) or an inaccurate conclusion that we need to fertilize the slow-to-leaf sago palm (thus disrupting its process), rushing to create something that doesn't feel aligned just causes stress and the need to double-back and try again.

Dormancy takes many forms in the plant world. For example, sometimes too much or too little water creates a type of dormancy, as the plant literally saves its energy to make it through the crisis. Resting is healing, so pushing through when we are ill prolongs the illness and may endanger our health. Indeed, when someone has been severely hurt physically, medical staff may decide to induce a coma, so the body can focus intensely on healing.

Surviving losses and trauma requires rest and healing, something we accept as obvious when we have a physical injury. Yet we may discount the impact of an emotional injury, or in the case of a physical or sexual assault, focus only on the physical healing and lock away the emotional injury until it makes us acknowledge it by upping the ante through anxiety, ruminations, physical symptoms, or sleep disturbances. Our mind and body will create the rest needed to heal, even if it means shutting down and limiting function.

Recognizing our need for rest and restoration before we're forced to confront it—and deal with a much more complex healing process—is simply living according to nature, and does not qualify for our societal judgment of laziness or unproductiveness.

Our need for daily, seasonal, and healing times of rest are intrinsic to our own unique Essential Nature, and both recognizing and honoring this—without judgment—can be the path to wellness and peace.

Yet even in the plant world, a healthy, well-sited plant can fall victim to illness or disease. When this happens, it is all the more crucial that it has the ability to respond quickly to cope with the symptoms. And it does! A plant doesn't try to "push through" and wait for a better time to tend to itself; it just mobilizes its defenses.

When humans encounter a physical illness—whether because we've neglected our health or simply because something invaded our otherwise robust immune system—we are often much more likely to think instead of act: "I don't have *time* to be sick right now!" or "I'll rest after I make dinner, finish the laundry, and email that report to my boss." Ironically, when we prioritize chores or deadlines over responding to illness, we often take longer to heal than if we had just listened to our body at the first sign of a problem. When it comes to disease response, plants are masters at self-care, as we'll see in the next chapter.

Key Takeaways — Harvest the Fruit:

- **Rest is a biological necessity, not a moral failure.** All living beings—including plants—require cycles of rest and dormancy to survive and thrive. Needing rest is not laziness; it is part of our Essential Nature.

- **Dormancy happens whenever conditions aren't supportive**—not just seasonally. Plants rest in response to stress, overwhelm, or lack of resources. Humans do the same when facing illness, trauma, exhaustion, or misaligned environments.

- **Modern culture and societal expectations can disrupt our natural rhythms.** Light pollution, screens, and hustle culture interfere with circadian cycles, sleep, and hormonal balance—undermining mental, emotional, and physical health.

- **Rest looks different for different beings and different seasons of life.** Some plants visibly shut down; others rest quietly beneath the surface. Likewise, some people need overt withdrawal, while others replenish internally without obvious signs.

- **Adaptation has limits—even for the most resilient.** Like mangroves facing climate change, humans who continually adapt without rest eventually reach a breaking point. Survival sometimes requires slowing growth and prioritizing self-preservation.

- **Liminal space—pausing between what was and what's next—is fertile ground.** Periods of uncertainty and stillness allow energy to consolidate, insight to emerge, and future growth to align more deeply with one's Essential Nature.

- **Honoring rest enables more meaningful, sustainable blooming.** When we respect our daily, seasonal, and healing cycles of rest, we protect our capacity to create, contribute, and thrive—again and again.

Reflection Questions — Plant New Seeds:

- What messages have shaped how you view rest and productivity, and how are they influencing your ability to pause or slow down right now?

- What signals from your body, emotions, or energy suggest that dormancy—or reduced growth—may be necessary in this season?

- If you trusted your Essential Nature, what kind of rest would you allow yourself, and what is one small, unapologetic way you could honor it this week?

CHAPTER 7 DISEASE:

How do you foster wellness and heal?

"The soul always knows what to do to heal itself. The challenge is to silence the mind."

— CAROLINE MYSS

"Healing may not be so much about getting better, as about letting go of everything that isn't you—all the expectations, all the beliefs—and becoming who you are."

— RACHEL NAOMI REMEN

Amazingly, plants can fight off certain diseases. They typically do this by recognizing quickly that something is attempting harm. At times, plants can actually communicate the impending harm to other plants! They often do this by releasing Volatile Organic Compounds (VOCs) from roots, stems, or leaves. These "infochemicals" act like smoke signals, alerting other plants to enact whatever protective mechanisms they have at their disposal to limit damage.

How does this translate to humans? Recognition, acceptance and communication.

Often when we feel unwell, we respond by denial or, equally as unhealthy, doubling down and ignoring our body's need for rest and healing. We often default to thinking of disease as a near-end state: something really serious or debilitating. However, the word "disease" comes from the Old French, meaning lack of ease. What if we shift our thinking a tiny bit and put a pause into the word: dis-ease? Perhaps if we think of it more broadly—as anything that gives us a sense of feeling "off"—we can address that feeling sooner, rather than waiting until our physical, emotional, or intellectual functioning is severely compromised.

When we face life situations where things feel weighty and suffocating, it can infect our entire being, as well as our relationships. Sometimes, when we first notice some stagnation, we might ignore it, thinking it will pass. But if we don't start injecting some fresh perspective into that space—in the form of curiosity, recognition of the "stuck" pattern, or even giving air to the problem—it will become increasingly heavy and it will, almost invariably, spread to healthy aspects of our bodies or relationships.

Powdery mildew, a common fungal disease, is a classic example of what happens to plants that don't have adequate air circulation. Roses are especially susceptible, although mildew does plague other plant species, including grapes (*Vitis*), cucumbers (*Cucumis*), garden phlox (*Phlox*), and lilacs (*Syringa*). Powdery mildew looks pretty much as the name suggests: leaves are covered with a white, powder-like substance. There are some organic solutions for arresting its spread, but knowledge and prevention are the best options. The fungus thrives, as fungi do, in damp conditions with little air flow. It spreads quickly if it's not addressed. Pruning (cutting off the infected parts) and increasing air circulation can help, but once the disease attacks, weekly spray treatments are often needed to stem the spread. Lack of vigilance allows powdery mildew to advance and compromise the overall health of the plant.

When we avoid difficult conversations or allow worries to languish in stagnant silence, "mildew" grows in our emotional world. Honest communication, movement, or reaching out for help are the human equivalents of fresh air. And giving air to concerns and issues is best done when the first signs of trouble are evident.

One solution for powdery mildew is to remove and dispose of infected leaves and stems to prevent further spread. While the infected stems and leaves will naturally wither and die on their own, pruning them out at the first sign of trouble limits the impact on the rest of the plant. Yet when we encounter issues in our own lives, it's often human nature to underestimate the danger, assuming the problem will just go away. And the longer we tolerate it, the more parts of ourselves or our relationship can die off, impacting our overall well being.

Powdery mildew also thrives in shade, so ensuring adequate sunshine is a potent preventive measure. If we feel too shaded—isolated, separated from the warmth of connection—we can sink into the heaviness of the mildew until it's difficult to move—physically or emotionally—and make our way into the sun to seek support.

Spacing plants adequately also helps prevent the infection of mildew. So for us, this may be the opposite of feeling too shaded, too distant from warmth and support. For some of us, it could mean that we feel too crowded, making it challenging to get enough of our own oxygen—enough independence or adequate solitude. If our Essential Nature thrives when we have space of our own, separate from others, including our partner at times, then too much intertwining or being planted too close feels like its own form of mildew: heavy and suffocating.

Finally, powdery mildew can overwinter or survive in discarded plant detritus so it's important to keep clippings cleaned up. A well-tended life, like a clean garden, helps us move out the trouble spots before they become overwhelming. And removing the diseased parts means we can't continue to revisit the same issues and drag them back into our garden, continuing the disease progression.

Again, the overall solution is directing your attention to any problem areas and giving air to your needs and your concerns. It is the one action that can start to lessen the heavy coating on your mind and heart.

Unfortunately, when diseases strike trees, the closeness of their forest community allows them to spread faster and more easily. It is said that we are most like the five people we spend the most time with. Surround yourself with healthy, open and positive relationships. This will lessen the chance that disease will occur, and increase the probability for a speedy, no-drama resolution with minimal impact.

Dutch elm disease is a deadly fungus that is spread primarily by European elm bark beetles. As is often the case, certain diseases and pests become a problem because they are transported to a geographical area with native plants and trees that do not have a natural resistance to the introduced threat. In the case of Dutch elm disease, it was first discovered in Holland, then transferred via diseased wood that was shipped to the United States. The native elm trees are quite susceptible, while the Asian species are less so. The disease sets in when the beetles feed on diseased wood, then carry the disease to healthy trees. When Dutch elm disease infects a tree, it cuts off the tree's ability to carry water to its branches and leaves, and eventually the branches wilt and the tree dies.

In a sense, overwhelming or chronic stress can block our energy, leading to less than optimal functioning of our emotional processing, memory, cognitive ability, or even our heart health. Recognizing the signs of blocked energy can allow time to apply options for healing.

Sometimes grafting healthy root stock onto the ailing tree can save it. As we explored in chapter 3, sometimes we need to bring in nutrients we are lacking by stretching our roots toward additional nutrients or by amending our soil. This might take the form of therapy, rest, medicine, or making changes to our diet, movement, and sleep.

When we encounter stressors, our body works to react, then restore itself. Our nervous system needs to complete the stress response cycle. For example, when we encounter acute, or short-term, intense stress, adrenaline is released and tells our sympathetic nervous system to prepare us to meet the challenge: increased heart rate, short, quick breathing, blood rushing to our extremities in case we need to flee or fight. Once the danger is past, we eventually reset back to a calmer baseline, aided by the parasympathetic (or calming) part of our nervous system.

In situations where our sympathetic nervous system fires up to meet a threat, but that threat doesn't occur—for example, we avoided a car accident—our bodies offload the physical stress through shaking, crying, or taking deep, gulping breaths. We didn't need the adrenaline to respond to the stressor through fighting or fleeing, so now the parasympathetic nervous system completes the cycle by offloading the excess energy.

Chronic stressors, like a long-term illness, unresolvable work-related issues, or poverty, typically do not allow the circuit to cycle and reset. We can't navigate through them quickly, then return to baseline. There doesn't seem to be an end to the stressor, so our sympathetic nervous system remains engaged. Eventually, this causes stuck energy, just like the disease that invaded the tree and spread. We have fewer options to work through the stress and reset because our physical and mental circuits are overloaded. The impact of chronic stressors can have an increasingly harmful impact, when we become acclimated to the situation and cease to recognize the increased consequences to our health.

The actions of humans can also increase the spread of Dutch elm disease. It can be spread by the use of gardening tools, like pruners, that are contaminated. This transfers the disease through careless practices.

Being vigilant in our lives regarding situations that are impacting us and causing strain is an important aspect of managing situations before they feel overwhelming. This can include setting boundaries or pruning the parts of our life that don't support healthy functioning.

Although potentially lethal, Dutch elm disease progresses rather slowly. That can often be the case with situations in life where we allow something new into our ecosystem because it seems fun or safe or novel. We may not allow ourselves to perceive the overall impact of it because the signs are subtle at first. If we experienced the end result at the beginning, we would much more easily recognize the toxicity.

We are often given clues to situations that require our attention. And it's typical to ignore the first few signs. We may think, "Maybe if I just ignore it, it will get better." Or we tell ourselves that we'll address it when we have more time.

Rewind to my thyroid cancer experience. I knew, when I felt that lump, that it shouldn't be there. That it was *not good.* I didn't ignore it; I got the message, loud and clear.

But in the short time leading up to my diagnosis, I had several people, including three from the medical community, tell me it was probably nothing. And while none suggested that I ignore it, I suppose I expected them to mirror my own inner alarm. My primary care doctor was probably the most dismissive. I'll never forget his words: "Everybody feels a lump and thinks they have cancer." But he dutifully sent me for an ultrasound. As I was lying there, neck exposed and feeling the pressure of the wand, I focused on the ceiling and pushed down the panicky feeling of being strangled.

Afterward, as I wiped the gel from my throat, I casually commented to the tech, "Yeah, my doctor said it was probably a cyst."

The tech's response? "Oh, it's not a cyst." And sent me on my way.

Sure enough, I was referred for a needle biopsy. That felt, weirdly, less invasive than the ultrasound because, even though a needle was repeatedly stabbing me in the throat, the area was numb—kind of like my emotions by that point.

I was, again, sent on my way with imaginary cartoon question marks trailing me down the hall and out to my car. My doctor called me that evening. His chagrin was evident in his voice. "The biopsy indicates that you have thyroid cancer."

Some people would not have made a doctor appointment so soon after feeling the lump as I did. They would have found solace in the assurances of others that "it's probably nothing." As we say in the therapy biz, "Denial ain't just a river in Egypt." But I knew, on some level, that it was something I needed to address as soon as possible. I knew I had to push through the fear to get an answer.

Looking for early signals of an issue and getting help quickly is imperative. Another consideration, however, is paying attention to the environment. In the case of organic farming, if you tend to the soil biome, it serves as a protective factor in the event there is an invasive disease, such as late blight, which can wipe out an entire tomato crop in days.

In the same way, a healthy gut biome is key to human health. I discovered I had habits that made my cancer more likely to grow. As mentioned before, we all have cancer cells in our bodies. A combination of genetics and lifestyle determine whether those cells remain in check or whether they find a food source and grow.

For myself, I firmly believe the cancer cells that grew and took hold in my body were partly influenced by my reluctance to fully use my voice. I allowed the world to decide how I should act in order to be acceptable, to be a "good girl." Since my diagnosis and recovery, I work to use my voice for my own good, as well as for supporting all women stepping into their full power and taking up their space.

Growing to the true specifications on our plant tag often requires pushing through hidden narratives and the fear that can arise when we step outside of socially acceptable gender-based behaviors. Our internal critic may start yapping, telling us we're "too much" or to "stay small." In the same way as black spot disease affects roses, making their leaves continually weaken until they drop, we can lose parts of ourselves if we succumb to internal messages that tell us to act in ways that keep us under the radar or make us "acceptable" under societal rules.

Black spot disease on rose leaves

Noticing the initial signs of the human version of black spot makes it easier to eradicate it before it *does* make us smaller. Each time we hear a negative message, it's like a spreading disease—tiny black spots slowly mask our most special traits. Parts of ourselves—usually, the most effervescent and sparkly parts—get lost, stuffed down until we can become just like rose bushes that are bred for easy growing. They all look the same and bloom reliably but have no scent. They are just facsimiles of the true originals.

Verticillium wilt can affect many types of trees, shrubs, and ornamental plants. The disease hides in the soil and, over time, it blocks a plant's vascular system. There's no way to eradicate it; verticillium wilt stays in the soil. But improving the health of the plants, including planting resistant varieties, and optimizing soil health, are key to plant survival in spite of the need to live with the vestiges of the dis-ease in their soil.

Old wounds or unprocessed grief may drain our emotional energy, like the devastating effects of verticillium wilt. We cannot undo what was done to us. But we can change the narrative. Instead of allowing situations to simply live in our everyday soil and circulate through our lives, we can solarize our soil (using the sun to reduce the disease in the soil) by allowing more positive energy, relationships, and freedom of self-expression into our lives.

In the plant world, we prune out infected branches to minimize the impact. For humans, this may mean recognizing what needs to be removed in order to allow healthy growth: a relationship, a job situation, a living arrangement, or even a disconnect from social media or other negative influences. In some cases, just like crop rotation is a preventive measure, removing yourself from certain environments can be a powerful fungicide.

One of the most damaging societal messages comes from the hustle culture, which emphasizes busyness over rest and a 24/7 work ethic. Seeing the lives of everyone on social media can lead to misinterpreting their road to success, their true level of achievement, and, most damaging, the mental and physical health costs of their success.

Plants recognize that trying to produce more and more seeds, just because that is one measure of plant success, is impossible. Even plants that are bred for higher yields sacrifice resilient traits of the mother plant—often, gene variety and natural disease resistance. Isn't that ironic?

A healthy work ethic is important to achieve goals, but being constantly on the go and continually reaching for the next thing can suffocate those parts of life that bring balance: connection, rootedness, and, of course, rest and mindfulness.

Root rot in plants is similar, and it can impact nearly any plant in the same way the strain of hustle culture affects many humans. But in this case, it's too much of a good thing—taking something we need to survive, or even thrive, and applying it to our life so liberally that we start to drown in it.

Root rot happens when there is too much moisture, resulting in root suffocation; the roots can no longer nourish the plant. Something that plant needs to thrive—water—has become the thing, in excess, that threatens its survival. In fact, over-watering a houseplant is probably one of the most common issues that kills them. Many people don't realize they are over-watering. We know it needs water to live, so we give it more. And more. And we nurture it to death! Because it often doesn't occur to us that what is life-sustaining in moderate amounts can be harmful in excess.

We can make that mistake ourselves, with exercise, medicine, or even supplements. We know we need to move to be healthy, but sometimes our bodies need a rest. And they try to tell us. But gym posters with slogans like "Pain is weakness leaving the body" convince us that health needs to hurt. Or we treat pain with an over-the-counter pain reliever and don't realize that over time, we are taking more and more of it. Or if one supplement can help us sleep, certainly doubling the dose can help us sleep *even better,* right? It's an herb—how dangerous can it be? Yet herbs are some of the most potent healers, and more is not better. In fact, like the genesis of root rot, we continue to feel the pain or the exhaustion, so we double down and do *more* of what we're already doing.

I used to get wicked migraines. They were often triggered by my menstrual cycle. What I didn't recognize for years was that oral contraceptives made the headaches worse. I'm talking about five straight days of migraines. I took an OTC pain reliever multiple times a day. After a while, it only blunted the pain enough for me to make it through a work day. When I finally came to my senses and realized I was giving myself the equivalent of root rot, I abruptly stopped the medicine. And believe me, the rebound pain was white hot. But that was my body adjusting.

Yes, it took time, and the real corner-turning didn't happen until I looked at my overall Essential Nature. I tracked my food, my sleep, my exercise and my pain through the stages of my cycle. It was certainly not a quick fix—similar to recovery in nature. Plants don't just bounce back from a disease. In the case of root rot, it may take digging them out of the ground (or their pot) and replanting them into soil that nourishes instead of suffocates. And even then, the plant will take some time to recover. After all, it almost died.

For my migraines, it took a long time to really make the changes that helped me feel painfree. And then, as is the case with women and aging, I hit perimenopause and my hormones decided to upend my system. But by now, I knew the signs. I didn't attempt a quick fix. I adjusted my eating— cutting back severely on sugar, alcohol, and unhealthy forms of fat—and I also adjusted my thyroid medicine.

A consistent focus on my overall health supports my immune system and limits my migraines. Yes, I still get them periodically. Times of high stress usually make me more vulnerable to an attack.

And for plants, too, stress increases vulnerability to disease. Too much rain? Root rot. Too much sun? Leaf scald. Simply planting a plant in the wrong spot (too much/too little sun, too wet/too dry soil) creates stress, which takes us right back to the beginning of this book. The right climate zone and an ideal site (sun/shade balance) is the difference between surviving and thriving.

It's complex, and sometimes we can fall into the trap of continuing to do more of what we're already doing, even though it doesn't work. As a client commented recently, "Continually doing the same thing and expecting a different result is the definition of insanity." (A version of this is often attributed to Albert Einstein, although it is more likely a paraphrasing of a line from a Rita Mae Brown novel.)

When a plant experiences overwhelm or dis-ease, it doesn't pretend it's okay. We can tell just by looking at its leaves, abundance of blooms, and growing habits whether it is struggling or not. Yet we ourselves conceal our own struggles while continuing to do more of what isn't working because we saw it work for someone else, we are misinformed about the effectiveness, or worst of all, we think there is something wrong with *us* because it isn't working.

Sometimes what ails us is an old wound that we continue to cover up, or try to treat with remedies that don't bring improvement, or that make it worse—like my taking too much pain medication. In a sense, those headaches were a mirror for a deeper wound. Migraines are actually an autoimmune issue. Even before my thyroid cancer diagnosis, my hormonal orchestra was woefully out of sync. I only focused on the pain in my head—I didn't realize that it was coming from a compromised gut biome and likely traumatic issues that I had stuffed into a compartment in my brain. Ironic that they came out in the form of headaches, huh?

My own experience, as well as countless clients' cases, continue to reinforce my belief that, when we have a physical malady, it's "stuck energy." We are electric—our heart runs on electrical signals. When we experience stressors, it's our body that needs to respond first. If we don't complete the cycle—allow the sympathetic nervous system to rev up to address it, then back off so the parasympathetic nervous system can reboot things and bring us back to baseline—the energy gets stuck.

My cancer cells took root at the base of my throat because that's where my energy was stuck: By ascribing to the expectation that nice girls smile and nod and pretend everything is fine, my body found a way to express something that I didn't allow my voice to express.

Wounds on trees can also lead to diseases that, if unchecked, will affect the health of the entire organism. When trees are pruned incorrectly, it can allow pathogens to invade the wound through the exposed vascular tissues. These diseases can be avoided by proper techniques, including knowing what to prune from the tree, and using clean tools. In trees, as in humans, sometimes wounds occur either by a traumatic event (storms, less than optimal growth) or well-meaning pruning efforts (cutting off the wrong parts or using the only tool available, even if it's dull or carrying disease).

Anthracnose affects sycamores, as well as other trees and plants. It is a fungal disease that largely affects new growth and appears as brown spots on young leaves. Although trees can recover and even put out leaf buds, anthracnose often creates sunken, spreading lesions that weaken fruit and leaves. Long *cankers* (dead spots) can appear on twigs and larger branches. Cutting out these spots using clean, sharp tools, preferably under the guidance of a certified arborist, is the key to preventing longterm effects to the health of the tree.

When we experience wounds, especially emotional wounds, we often want them to heal as quickly as possible. However, if they aren't tended to fully or completely or we try to heal them without help, they can, indeed, become like dead spots. They may affect our ability to find healthy attachment to partners, or they may short-circuit our attempts to overcome anxiety related to the source of the wound.

Often, when wounds occur in childhood, we survive but in a compromised state, similar to the sycamore surviving anthracnose. And the longer we allow the emotional canker to solidify and affect our overall functioning, the larger the impact can be on our ability to thrive and take up our full space in the world.

We may find healing on our own, but at times, it takes a trained human arborist (aka therapist or coach) to help us address and repair deeper wounds.

Sometimes simply allowing ourselves to see the wound and name it—through meditation, journaling, radical acceptance, and grace—is the first step to finding health and wholeness. What can make this difficult is a human spirit compromised by years spent trying to live in spite of the canker—to continually circumvent the scarred aspects of ourselves.

In the same way as anthracnose enters through a compromised trunk and spreads, fire blight is a bacterium that enters through a wound and spreads. Occurring largely in apple and pear trees, the symptoms include blackening of blossoms, new growth, and branches. It appears as if the plant was scorched by fire.

Long term stressors, like chronic illness, an abusive or simply unhealthy relationship, poverty, or other situations that we need to endure over time, can lead to burnout. Again, we can't complete the stress cycle. Inside, we may feel like that plant with fire blight: blackened and scorched, exhausted and charred.

Recovery begins by finding ways to prune out the disease. Depending on the stressors, this can seem overwhelming or even impossible. If we have a child with special needs or are in a relationship from which we can't immediately leave, we can start with where we have control: our internal landscape.

Finding ways to grow around the scars is a start. Reaching out for help—for yourself or the loved one for whom you're caring—is often a secondary thought, as we allow our internal beliefs to stop us: "I got myself into this. I should be able to handle this. What if they think it's my fault?"

Recognizing that these aren't incontrovertible truths is an important step. Test the evidence. What makes your belief true? Is it just because someone you trusted in your early life *told* you it was true? Ask yourself if you would judge someone you love in the same way you are judging yourself. Or consider whether you would treat someone you love in the way that a friend, partner, or loved one is treating you. Then trust yourself to take steps to lessen your own dis-ease.

A plant tries its very best to extricate itself from situations that are hurting it. It does not—cannot!—question whether it deserves to be well or whether creating a canker as a temporary means of protection was stupid. It does its best. Just as we all do.

Trying to connect to the parasympathetic nervous system—the part that de-escalates our cortisol response of shallow breathing, tenseness, rapid heartbeat, or palpitations, breathlessness, and wicked ruminations—is imperative. In most situations, it won't be a quick fix. But finding even five minutes a few times a day to be in nature or sit quietly and focus on breathing is a start. Those seemingly insignificant practices give our brain and body a break and allow tiny, new growth to start.

There are times we all think, "How did I end up here?" We tend to seek out familiar situations, even if, historically, those similar situations were unhealthy. If we grew up in a chaotic home, we might seek out romantic relationships or friendships that often feel volatile or explosive.

It's not uncommon to feel unsettled by a calm or quiet environment. Peace can freak us out—the silence allows too much time to hear our own *inner* chaos.

Seeking a more peaceful existence often starts with changing your environment. Like a recovering addict, we may need to push back against the urge to find the people, places, and things that support our addiction to an unhealthy ecosystem. But chaos cannot survive in an environment devoid of the aspects that contribute to it.

We can't always eradicate diseased or unhealthy situations from our original environment, but we can resist carrying diseased beliefs and attachment issues to our own chosen environment. Although sometimes it may feel easier just to allow the infection to spread into our next life stage, there are options.

Cedar-apple rust is an example of a plant disease that spreads to a new environment, requiring two different hosts. It is a fungus with a two-year lifecycle that requires invasion of an initial host—the Eastern red cedar—where it overwinters. In spring, it transfers to an apple (or related) tree species to complete its life cycle. Similar to having a childhood environment or other early situation with unhealthy aspects, the rust begins by creating brown galls—abnormal growths—on this primary cedar species. The galls swell and break open after winter and repeatedly produce orange, jelly-like horns during the rains of spring. These horns then shrink and expand with varying rainfall. They look a bit like the alien enemy in a horror movie.

Rust spores form on the gelatinous masses. They cannot further infect the primary host, but the rainfall helps them spread to apple and crabapple trees, where yellow lesions eventually appear on the leaves. As the disease progresses, the leaves with the yellow spots will develop raised orange lumps that begin to ooze and eventually turn black. (See? Horror movie.) Eventually, spores are produced that again invade the original cedar host, completing the life cycle and re-igniting the process of infection.

Although this disease may seem debilitating, many trees continue living with the disease. Humans, as well, can find ways toward balance and fulfillment. In the same way that plants growing in the most supportive environment can better withstand damage, we may create a life large and robust enough to accommodate (and lessen) the impact of a compromised origin.

When a more impactful solution is needed, pruning the affected branches from the tree affected by rust is an option. Similarly, ending relationships (even cutting familial ties), changing jobs, moving to a new city, or making healthier food choices can disrupt the cycle and create a healthier life.

The more support and healthy connections we have in our life, the less the old patterns can take hold. This disease, in particular, needs a very specific host to continue to grow and invade. In the absence of this, it becomes innocuous.

Taking any step toward peace and thriving can feel unfamiliar and strange. That discomfort doesn't mean it's the wrong decision or that you're making bad choices. You just need to adapt to a new environment, even as you recognize it is where you truly belong.

When a plant needs to withstand strong winds, its growth is affected. Perhaps its trunk is bent, or there are only leaves on the leeward side of the tree. If we could magically create a windbreak for that tree, it would eventually leaf out more evenly and create strong, straight growth above the compromised trunk. Those impacts—past times of dis-ease—become part of the tree, just like our experiences are part of our Essential Nature. They don't make us less beautiful. They show us how far we've come. They are a testament to an inspiring life narrative.

Now that we've addressed disease (internal challenges) and healing, let's explore pests (external challenges) and boundaries.

Key Takeaways — Harvest the Fruit:

- **Plants model early warning and communication.** They can recognize threats quickly and even "warn" neighboring plants through chemical signals (VOCs), prompting protective responses. The human parallel is noticing early signs, accepting them, and communicating rather than denying.

- **"Disease" can be reframed as "dis-ease"**—a loss of ease that deserves early attention. If we treat feeling "off" as meaningful data (not weakness), we can intervene sooner—before functioning or well being is severely compromised.

- **Stagnation spreads—fresh air heals.** Powdery mildew thrives in damp, airless conditions; emotionally, stuck patterns grow when worries and conflicts stay unspoken. Honest conversation, movement, and reaching out for help are the human equivalent of airflow.

- **Environment and community shape health**—for better or worse. Like diseases spreading more easily in dense forests, stress and dysfunction can spread through close networks. Choosing supportive relationships and healthy ecosystems reduces "infection" and supports recovery.

- **Chronic stress creates "blocked circulation."** When the nervous system can't complete the stress cycle, energy gets stuck, impacting mood, cognition, and the body. Resetting requires tools that support the parasympathetic system, not more pushing.

- **Some conditions can't be erased, but they can be managed**—and narratives can be changed. Like soil-borne diseases that remain present, we may not undo old wounds or origins, but we can strengthen resilience, choose supportive environments, and reduce impact through intentional care.

- **Pruning is protection, not punishment.** Sometimes healing means removing what's infected—beliefs, habits, relationships, jobs, or environments—so life energy can circulate again. Small daily practices (time in nature, grounding, breathwork) can help foster new, healthy growth.

Reflection Questions — Plant New Seeds:

- What feels stagnant, unresolved, or heavy right now (relationships, habits, beliefs, environments), and what might need fresh air or careful pruning to protect your wellbeing?

- How do you notice dis-ease affecting your body, mood, or thinking?

- What small, compassionate practices or supports help restore ease and circulation for you—and what is one step you can take this week to invite more of that in?

How do you create boundaries?

"Walls keep everyone out. Boundaries

teach them where the door is."

— MARK GROVES

"'No' is a complete sentence."

— ANNIE LAMOTT

Similar to disease response, some plants have natural attributes that protect them from pests, allowing them to respond to attacks and even heal from those attacks. For example, while the milkweed species (*Asclepias*) is the host plant for the monarch butterfly caterpillar, it is toxic to certain other insects and animals. In this way, it protects itself from becoming lunch for random animals, yet welcomes pollinators to its flowers when they bloom. Other plants have nectar that attracts ants to facilitate pollination, but that will kill other insects that could damage the plant.

Monarch butterfly on milkweed (Asclepias)

Each plant species has specific pests that it's susceptible to and unique ways of protecting itself that typically correspond to the weakness of the attacking pest. In the same way, our Essential Nature includes traits that make us susceptible to being influenced by the behavior of others or by the emotional tone of specific situations.

For example, if you are wired to be a caretaker and your early environment required that someone step into the caring role that was vacated by another, you may have taken on responsibilities that shaped who you are now. If you had an absent parent, due to a job, disinterest, or death, you may have fallen into a parentified role, even if you had another parent that was still present. Many times, the genetic aspect of our Essential Nature makes it nearly effortless to fall into the role in a family system aligning with that. We often assume the roles informed by that element of our nature when we are too inexperienced to make a conscious choice. And like a plant that simply leans toward the situation that will allow it to survive, we take on the role that ensures our own survival and, sometimes, that of our ecosystem.

Because I was the poster child for The Good Girl, the "nature" aspect of my personality, in concert with the environmental, or "nurture" aspect of my family, contributed to my drive to be a high achiever. I did my best not to make waves, and I tolerated living within the small emotional space left for my siblings and me after our brother's addiction absorbed most of our parents' energy. I was also raised in the Catholic faith, and got consistent admonishments from my dad about "compromising myself" soon after I started my first serious romantic relationship in high school.

Here's the thing, though: While my nature was wired to do the right thing, it was based on my conscience, not the Ten Commandments. It always made sense to me to be the best person I could be and treat other people as I would want to be treated. My natural empathy level often left my own heart battered when I witnessed the pain of others. But I had opinions, and my reluctance to create tension was often at odds with my desire to take a stand and point out blatant cruelty or inequality. But it was always easier to speak up in support of others than it was to defend my own needs and beliefs and to set boundaries.

The first time these two aspects of myself collided—the socially-acceptable good girl and the honest, practical girl—remains a crystal clear memory. It happened when I was in my early teens. My parents, my younger sister, and I were visiting my brother and his then-wife, and he was doing his typical drunken antics: pacing and ranting. Even then there was a part of me that recognized that the rules my parents had for him were different than they were for the rest of us. It wasn't the fault of my parents, to be honest. I believe they had no idea what to do with him, and so handled him with a mixture of guilt, fear, and morbid horror at what had become of their golden-skinned, bright little boy.

It was obvious to me that he was being an asshole. And that behavior, from any of the rest of us, would be instantly and firmly addressed. But add alcohol to the mix and it felt like the world shifted to some alternative existence where we were all looking at the ground while stones rained down on our heads. It felt ludicrous. So for the first of many times in my life, my mouth decided the fate of the rest of my person. I dared to take a stand.

What I said was, "Why don't you get off your fucking high horse and shut up?" To be honest, I don't even remember what caused *that* retort to his behavior, but I can only imagine he was belittling someone—me?—and I had had enough.

I was sent to wait in the car with my sister, and we sat in silence, holding hands in the back seat. When my parents came out and we began the short drive home, my dad glanced at me in the rearview mirror and told me that my behavior disappointed him.

Oof. I don't think I need to tell you the lesson I took from that. My good girl nature is acceptable. My practical nature, where my bullshit meter resided, was unacceptable. That behavior by an abusive drunk man was given a limitless pass, while a rational (albeit profane) observation of the destructiveness and inappropriateness of that same behavior by a high achieving, sensitive young woman was a disappointment.

I temporarily veered from the tolerant, quiet child my dad expected me to be, and he expressed his disappointment. Simple and direct. No expression of understanding of what it was like to be the one to whom the abuse and cruelty was often directed. To be honest, I'm not sure my dad even realized that my brother was abusive to me, but grossly underestimating his impact on every other member of the family seems inconceivable. Yet people live in much more logic-defying situations every single day.

It took quite a long time for me to sort that out—along with all the other emotional detritus that accompanies being a sibling of the sick kid who gets all the allowances. Part of my work was determining where my boundaries needed to be. It was quite easy with my brother. After his abuse transferred to his own family, and I went away to college and got perspective, I made a hard line. Even when he moved back in with my mom, after my dad died, I told my mom that while I understood her choice, I didn't agree with it. I told her I would love to see her as much as she wanted, but I would not visit her while he lived there. By that point, I had a career, was living on my own, and felt no qualms about that decision. Other boundaries along the way were harder to suss out, but cruelty, abuse, and the victim mindset were a clear and obvious hard, "No," and my boundaries reflected that. Blood is not thicker than the line I took against abuse and cruelty.

In this way, I feel like the milkweed. Being a host plant means some degree of destruction, and the survival of monarchs depends, literally, on finding patches of this on their flight to and from Mexico each year. The viscous milky juice of its leaves protects it from any other feeders. It is created to support the survival of the monarch. Yet it shares the gift of pollen from its flowers freely. This ensures its own survival.

To me, milkweed makes a firm, hardline boundary. No apologies. I learned early and indelibly that there are people for whom I will sustain a degree of damage: the normal give and take and misunderstandings that actually enrich a loving relationship. There are no bonds—family, friend, or romantic—that do not involve disagreements and unintentional hurts. But a relationship with careless, apathetic, or blatantly hurtful behavior that wants no tempering or consequence? Nope.

In my work, I do my best to give help and unconditional positive regard to clients who are struggling with addictions or mental health issues that mirrored my brother's challenges. I think of the help I give to them as one of the ways I pollinate. Offering care is a renewable resource for me, and any healing that happens only enriches the ecosystem. I endure no burden, as long as I stay healthy. However, if I allowed anyone access to my own structure—the leaves of my being—that would most certainly create damage that may not be survivable.

Other plants have external *do not enter* signs. Roses have vicious thorns that protect the plant from animal munching, but their leaves and flowers are often assailed by diseases, as discussed previously. Roses have one of the most extensive lists of potential pests of nearly any plant species. Among the list of potential assailants are Japanese beetles, aphids, thrips, mites, scale, rose leafhopper, and rose slugs. Thorns are an example, in this case, of much bluster but little protection.

There are times when we encounter humans who have thorns too. These are often the people for whom we tack on the phrase, "until you get to know them." For example, "She's kind of a witch … until you get to know her."

I imagine these people developed a thorny exterior because they were taken advantage of too often along the way. People were drawn to their softness, perhaps, but ended up causing damage. So they armed themselves with a harsh exterior that may do little once they again trust the wrong person. Allowing others to display their defenses initially, yet remaining patient when we glimpse attractive features emerging underneath the prickly exterior can result in lifelong, mutually supportive relationships.

Unfortunately this outer human defense can be too effective. Developed to protect a soft heart, it can block others' ability to see beyond it. I had a young female client that remains one of my all-time favorite students from my long career. She was sarcastic, funny, and often irreverent. She engendered trust from adults, but invariably stumbled into trouble and wasted some of the goodwill equity she had earned.

Coming from an inner-city, working class family, she had developed a rough exterior due to dysfunction and abuse, but to me, it was obviously a protective adaptation. Her genetic Essential Nature was sensitive and empathic. Her exterior developed like calluses do, from necessity, built up from years of friction as a response to the tender pain of a blister.

At one point, yet again fallen from the good grace of adults and in a manipulative romantic relationship, she sat in my office in tears. Through sobs, she told me she was having suicidal thoughts and she asked, "How can my friends and my parents not understand how much I'm hurting?" After a pause, I asked her if she *told* people that she was hurting. (No.) When her parents asked her how school was going, how did she answer? (Fine.) Did she clearly tell the boy who she loves (that doesn't love her) that she no longer wanted a sexual relationship with him? (No.) Did she allow peers to see that she was a good-hearted, caring potential friend versus a flippant, sarcastic smart-mouth? (No.)

All those layers, those calluses designed to protect her, were so effectively painful to get past that very few people saw her gifts beneath her rough exterior. They felt rebuffed instead, and decided there wasn't anything softer or redeeming underneath.

One of the most powerful boundary setters in the plant world is the black walnut tree (*Juglans nigra*). It utilizes allelopathy (which literally translates as "death to others"), a means of protecting itself from other plant species, by exuding the chemical *juglone*. The walnut tree wages chemical warfare with adjacent plants by releasing juglone into the soil and poisoning the roots of other plants. Or so some believe.

Black walnut (Juglans nigra) leaf, hull, and shell

When I was trained as a Master Gardener, we were taught that extreme care needed to be exercised when choosing plants to install under walnut trees. However, some studies indicate there is conflicting data regarding how damaging walnut trees' chemicals really are to neighboring plants. As it turns out, many of the warnings are based on anecdotal data from farmers and gardeners, and the harm to adjacent plants may have been attributable to other factors. When actual chemical testing was done with the leaves, bark, and shells of the walnuts, the evidence was not compelling. Further, healthy soil can neutralize that potential damage. Yet the cautionary tales persist. This is an example of a boundary that is, in large part, fallacious.

Everyone needs support at times. Yet when we need to toughen up—to develop calluses or other protection to survive our environment—we can forget to show people our genetic (more vulnerable) Essential Nature underneath. We develop the strength to adapt to a harsh environment, but fail to recognize that a new environment, or people who come into our life later, may not require us to maintain the same intensity of self-protection. Or we don't know how to ask for help because the ecosystem where we were first planted didn't give us what we needed. It hurt us instead.

And sometimes, we can feel like the tall, impervious walnut tree, spreading our subterranean poison to keep everyone at bay. We can come by the poison quite by mistake: It can develop from the belief that people don't *want* to help because the ones that were supposed to didn't. Like parents. Or teachers. Or pastors. Or any adult that we're taught to believe will protect us … if they love us.

And that poison can hurt us most of all, because it often comes from a belief that, "If only I was a better son or a more compliant daughter or a stronger (fill in your own word), things would have been different." There's the beginning of the juglone: "I will never give people a chance to move in and hurt me again." And somewhere inside of us, it becomes a self-fulfilling prophecy. We have created such an inhospitable ecosystem that nothing can grow—which conversely confirms our irrational belief that nothing *wants* to grow because we're just an unlovable plant.

When we experience hurt or disappointment or abandonment, it's tempting to believe we don't need anyone. That we can find everything we need within ourselves. That we can't trust our community to support us because it hasn't in the past. But guess what? Plants protect each other. We are made, hormonally, to support each other too. Remember oxytocin, the cuddle hormone? It surges when we exchange physical affection and offer emotional support. We are made to live in a community. And when we find the type of community we need—all the ways we discussed previously to allow our Essential Nature to guide us to our niche—we will discover the main key to thriving.

It can be tempting to focus on the people who didn't help or who created deep scars. But they are nature too. Perhaps they were living in a situation where they didn't get what they needed, so they aren't able to bloom in a way that sustains the seeds they create. Or they never got nutrients, whether from ill-formed roots or lack of nourishment, when they were planted.

Whatever led to your defenses against real and imagined foes, it is never too late to realign the boundaries you want and need based on what your Essential Nature wants to allow into your life. This may mean reflecting on all the other aspects of living like a plant—starting with your Thrivability Zone and what type of connection enriches you.

Stripping away all boundaries isn't the answer. It is simply the opposite side of the coin: While it isn't healthy to develop boundaries so impenetrable that we can't get or don't allow support by others, we also cannot fully abdicate our own ability to set limits—to create boundaries that are effective, permeable to support, and flexible.

If you've been thinking, "Dang, I actually need to have *more* juglone in my life, not less!" you're definitely not alone. Because what I have seen most often in my therapy practice is the polar opposite the walnut tree. Clients give and give until they have no idea where their needs start and the needs of everyone around them end.

Sheila, a composite of dozens of my clients, grew up in a home with a harsh and judgmental mother and a philandering father. Empathy is a central trait of her Essential Nature; she is literally wired as a connector. People like Sheila default to believing that harsh judgments by others, especially parents, are true. So she internalized her mom's pronouncements of her as "selfish" or "lazy," and spent most of her life trying to overcome a false narrative. Anyone who knows Sheila knows she is neither selfish nor lazy, but Sheila believed her mom. As we often do. I mean, she's the parent, right? Who would know our true nature better than the people that raised us?

Here's the thing: A large majority of the time, we don't see the connection between these early messages and our behavior. So Sheila's mission was to be as helpful and dutiful as she could, because she believed this was the only way to make her mom happy—to be a daughter worthy of love. (Spoiler: This is a losing battle.) As we began our work together, I knew she had fewer boundaries than a row of tender, unprotected lettuce seedlings in a field of rabbits. And now, Sheila is an adult, with a husband and kids. And mom is still part of her life.

Sheila is someone who will literally give you the shirt off your back—as well as her bra, if you really need it. You might imagine that her kids and her husband adore her. Well, they do. But often she drives them crazy, anticipating every need. To kids, that can sometimes feel nagging and suffocating. And it deprives them of learning from nature's lessons by trying and failing. Her husband? Well, a good guy, but he has no idea what she really wants or needs because she never told him. She spent her life taking that big, giving heart and trying to fit into all the different shapes she thought the people around her wanted.

Why did Sheila end up in my office? She was depressed. And she was anxious. See, when we keep doing the same thing and think we're going to get a different result, it creates anxiety. And when it dawns on us that our efforts aren't making us feel more worthy or providing gratitude from those around us, it's depressing. And, no surprise, she was having stomach issues and frequent migraines. Her body finally got involved.

If Sheila was a plant, she would barely be hanging on. She was pushing herself to continually flower, believing she had to constantly give to be a valuable part of the ecosystem, and she was not getting the nutrients she needed to sustain all that output. Her flowers weren't noticed anymore because she gave them constantly—too much of a good thing. She was offering nectar and pollen to insects that don't want or need it, and worse, they just kept taking without giving back. Remember, pollination is designed to be mutually beneficial. So when all manner of flies and bees and beetles use what you offer and give nothing in return, we call that a *parasitic relationship*.

As her therapist, the starting point with Sheila was to assess all the things we've discussed in this book: First, did she feel aligned with her zone? What type of roots did she have, and what nutrients were lacking in her soil? What was her ideal site—where did she find energy and joy? (This took some introspection, as she believed that her energy should be constant and that her only joy was bringing joy to others.) What was her dormancy cycle? How did she rest? (Only after everyone's needs were met. Read: rarely).

By helping Sheila see herself as a plant, she was more easily able to accept that she wasn't being "selfish" or "lazy" because, like nature, she had her own needs. And the rules of nature say that no being, especially plants, can continually grow only in a way that benefits their ecosystem without factoring in their own needs.

Sheila decided she could be an orchid. As we learned in chapter 1, they are stunning and a bit exotic. The thing about orchids that made them a good teaching plant for Sheila is that they certainly bring joy to those that experience their flower gifts, but they only allow access to certain pollinators. Some orchids are self-pollinating, an important reminder for those learning to recognize their own needs and make self-care a non-negotiable part of thriving.

There are somewhere between 28,000 and 30,000 known species of orchids—the largest family of flowering plants in the world—and they can be found on every continent. Their specific adaptations to their unique microclimates and ecosystems make them masters of managing boundaries.

We know that orchids, as a species, are pollinated by preferred pollinators, and that they often use *mimicry*: Some orchid flowers' appearance resembles female bees or wasps to entice the males of their preferred pollinators to their blooms to ensure the job gets done. There is even an orchid population on an island in the Indian Ocean where specific orchid species are pollinated only by crickets. Further, their flowers have an architecture that prohibits species of insects outside their preferred pollinators from accessing their valuable pollen.

This level of specificity—aka strategic boundary-setting—means that they put their energy into relationships that are mutually sustaining and that support their Essential Nature. They don't let just any ol' pollinator into their inner sanctum. By being selective, they get the support they need and, in turn, share their energy with those that want and need it.

We circled back to pollination and blooming for a minute because so often, the gifts we share with the world are impacted by the pests that show up (or that we allow) and threaten our ability to thrive. Orchids, as we've been discussing, are some of the most sought after flowers for collectors. Their amazing blooms would be nearly non-existent if they allowed any old bug or bat to tromp all over them. They know that they need to keep their social circle small and sustainable.

So you may be sitting there thinking it would be nice to be an orchid, but you believe you have pests in your environment that would be hell-bent on doing the tromping. And you already have the sense that you would have a hard time keeping them *from* tromping.

You're not wrong. No plant recovers instantaneously after it is transplanted from a space that challenges survival to a spot that supports thriving. Even when a plant is transferred to a much more hospitable environment, there is a period of adjustment. Roots need to establish and find new sources of nourishment, damage from the wrong site needs to be healed, and a new source of pollination, as well as community support, needs to be established. These are hardships, for sure. And a stressed plant—say it with me—is a vulnerable plant.

Aspects of your ecosystem will want you to stay put. They like their unlimited access. Here's where you take a page from the plant's book: First, plants don't feel guilty, so if that's an aspect limiting your boundary-setting, live like a plant! Emotions are transient. As my own therapist used to say, "Fear is just False Evidence Appearing Real."

When bark beetles start to invade a pine tree by burrowing into its bark, the tree pushes out a sticky resin to literally drown the intruders. That tree doesn't wait and debate; it doesn't need to reason with the beetles or plead. And it *certainly* doesn't think, "Well, maybe just this once ..." There is too much at stake. It acts swiftly and with certainty.

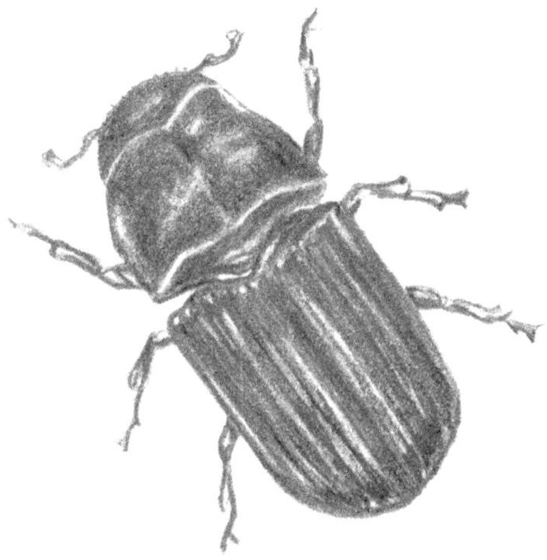

Bark beetle

A pine tree instinctively knows that the bark beetle is dangerous. When we encounter a person or a situation that is threatening our wellbeing, we nearly always sense it. Just like a tree. But depending on our socialization, we may talk ourselves out of making a boundary to protect ourselves.

In the case of Sheila, unconscious scripts ran in her brain. Her belief system was programmed by her natural, genetic tendency to care-take, and her early environment capitalized on this tendency through the behaviors of significant people in her early life. She believes, even if she isn't aware of it, that she needs to make sure everyone else is okay or else she is "selfish." She needs to keep going, keep smoothing the path in front of everyone else, even when she's tired, or else she's "lazy."

Finally, when Sheila's physical body reflected her overwhelming anxiety and depression, she was ultimately forced to ask for help. Only through reprogramming her beliefs to reflect what was true was she able to recognize she was acting against her best self-interest, as well as that of her entire ecosystem. The coping strategies she developed as a child, based on her Essential Nature, no longer functioned to protect her. Instead, they were impacting her survival.

Tuning into her Essential Nature and recognizing that the strategies of plant thriving apply to her, also, was the necessary first step to learning how and when to set boundaries. The ultimate step was to enact these new boundaries without over-reacting, like the walnut tree theoretically tends to do. Recognizing that she can step into a mutually supportive relationship within her ecosystem and allow *herself* to be supported by others—to be an equal member of the community—is the ultimate symbiosis of setting boundaries.

Remember that plants release VOCs (phytochemicals) that call in reinforcements if they are under attack. Both the corn plant (*Zea mays*) and the tomato plant *(Solanum lycopersicum)* release chemical S.O.S. when they are under attack by caterpillars. The cavalry comes, in the form of parasitic wasps, that specifically target the pests. Parasitic wasps lay their eggs on the caterpillars, which are slowly desiccated and die from the feeding larvae.

Our human form of VOCs is our voice. Sometimes just three small words, "I need help," can be tremendously difficult to push through our lips. But when we do, change can begin—even if it starts as a whisper.

As often happens in nature, mounting a defense is not a quick process. But as we learn how to reach out and request help, we slowly adjust to withstand the invader as our intervention takes hold.

While our supporters may not directly attack the people in our lives that are creating a toxic environment, they help us to neutralize the threat. We may decide to finally stop pretending everything is fine when we talk to our friend, we might enlist the help of a coach or a therapist, or we might talk with a supervisor about setting limits with our work load.

In the same way that companion planting—putting plants side-by-side that may attract the same insect pests—helps deter invaders from solely focusing on the flowers of one species, having a support system to share responsibilities with can lessen the load of everyday issues that may deplete our energy. Planting nasturtiums beside sunflowers shares the burden, as pesky aphids will, theoretically, divide their efforts and reduce the strain on the individual plants. Similarly, sharing tasks with other people helps each person better maintain their balance in the face of the stressors that can become heavy to navigate alone.

Even with all the reasons we can find to connect to the needs of our Essential Nature when battling our own pests and setting boundaries, we may often be tempted to revert back to our old habits. In fact, it's not uncommon for our boundaries to erode over time. This is a risk specifically as we are learning where we want to draw our lines, because this is when we are most likely to get pushback and be tempted to ease our guilt by restoring the former (unhealthy) ecosystem.

Plants in the cabbage family (*Brassicas)* produce bitter compounds called glucosinolates, which help repel invaders. Yet some pests adapt, making this barrier less effective. In the same vein, we may need to periodically re-assess our own boundaries, especially at certain times of the year. Perhaps holidays are a time when there are more people or situations that can push your boundaries, or increased activities and gatherings can deplete you more quickly. Additionally, when we or someone we love experiences a loss or trauma, we need to adjust our barriers to allow more or less infiltration, as needed.

Improving our wellbeing can boost the hardiness of our entire ecosystem. Just as one robust plant creates a healthier environment overall, by example, we empower others to reinforce their own health limits. Plants don't rely on

VOCs solely for their own defense; this is also a means of communication to alert their sister and brother plants that an attack is at hand.

So that supervisor I told you about way back at the beginning of this whole thing? Well, when my emotional and mental walls were breached by this person, my body responded before my brain caught up. My body knew that it was under attack. My brain was still trying to reason.

Because we are socialized to get along and blame ourselves, it took my brain a long time to accept what my body already sensed. When it finally did, it frantically tried to reason through the situation. And one of the steps I took was talking to the people in my ecosystem. Some of them? Well, their brains hadn't caught up yet, either, so they seemed unfazed. There was also a sense of danger—a fear—about speaking up. Remember the *Mimosa pudica*, the sensitive plant that wilts and plays dead to avoid getting munched on? There were a lot of *Mimosa pudica* reactions in my tight community; this was not something we had needed to defend against in our previous ecosystem.

As I worked through the situation, a few of my colleagues and I communicated in a manner similar to those plants that send out invisible VOCs. Big Brother was watching, but we supported each other in whatever ways we could, and eventually, we were able to migrate to safer soil and again find a climate that helped us recover and, eventually, thrive.

Sometimes it takes longer for certain plants to succumb to the threat. Nearly two years after I moved to a more hospitable environment (as did nearly all my closest colleagues), someone who seemed immune to the toxins at the time—we'll call her Amanda—-called me on the phone. Out of the blue. Amanda reached out to me because she remembered what happened to me, but she thought she was protected or even immune from the threat. She had felt the pressure, but at the time, she blamed herself. Because it felt similar to what she had experienced in a past toxic relationship, she believed she was over-reacting to familiar triggers.

Sometimes we are so used to trying to pull nutrients from depleted or compromised soil that we don't even recognize how much we're struggling. Or worse, we attribute it to weakness instead of deep awareness.

What finally helped Amanda see that she was trying to grow in an inhospitable environment? When other plants fade or die, the invader will move on to the ones left standing. And in this case, it eventually reached Amanda. Just as plants don't need to justify their behavior in protecting themselves, the most ruthless pests don't apply morals and conscience to their actions. They behave based on the programming of their Essential Nature. But it's never too late to find support from the community. Amanda said she called me because she instinctively felt she would be supported and seen. She knew I had experienced the same impact, and I had shared a warning.

Even if I wanted to defend myself like the pine tree with the invasive bark beetle, drowning someone in sticky sap can be frowned upon in the workplace. That's one reason we all need allies in our ecosystem. We use our VOCs to warn others and be ready to help when needed.

Whether you are experiencing a threat to your professional purpose or situation or you are finally taking up your space and creating boundaries in your personal life, there are people watching who may very well stand taller and stronger because they saw you do it.

Setting boundaries in your life will empower others to follow your example. And, ever so important: When you enact boundaries that require others to stop expecting you to solve their problems, you will make them resilient in their own way. Simply spraying pesticides doesn't allow plants to utilize their own defenses. Fighting pests *for* a plant doesn't allow it to learn to ask for help or develop its VOCs.

There's a concept in organic farming: *Integrated Pest Management* (IPM). This means utilizing a vast network of inputs to mimic an ecosystem, like introducing natural predators versus simply spraying toxic pesticides at the first sign of trouble. Or, more damaging, spraying those toxins as a preventive. Pesticides are used as a last resort. IPM is trusting nature, with a bit of a boost from us, to mount its own defenses when threatened. It's believing in the rhythm and balance of nature to take care of its own.

In the same way, we can trust our Essential Nature to inform us where we need to tighten our boundaries to limit harmful or parasitic impacts that can threaten vigor. And, when warranted, we can relax our heightened defenses and allow our ecosystem to foster relationships built on mutualism. No plant—and no human—exists as a truly solitary being, nor does it thrive by sacrificing its wellbeing for the larger community. Appropriate and flexible boundaries empower a true capacity for growth.

Key Takeaways — Harvest the Fruit:

- **Every being has natural defenses—and vulnerabilities—shaped by their Essential Nature.** Just as plants have specific pests and corresponding protections, humans have traits that make us sensitive in certain environments and resilient in others.

- **Early survival roles can become outdated defenses.** Roles like caretaker, peacekeeper, or "good girl" often develop to ensure survival in early ecosystems—but without reassessment, they can later undermine wellbeing.

- **Healthy boundaries are selective, not extreme.** Effective boundaries protect against harm while still allowing nourishing connection—like milkweed welcoming monarchs but deterring other feeders.

- **Some defenses are too weak, others too strong.** Thorns that look intimidating may send the wrong message without being truly protective, while overly rigid barriers (like imagined juglone) can isolate us from the very support we need.

- **Asking for help is a form of self-defense, not weakness.** Plants release VOCs to summon allies; humans do the same through voice, honesty, and reaching out to community.

- **Giving without reciprocity leads to depletion.** Constant caregiving without receiving nourishment creates parasitic dynamics that shift us from thriving to mere survival.

- **Boundaries evolve and require ongoing maintenance.** Just as pests adapt, life circumstances change—requiring us to revisit, strengthen, or soften boundaries across seasons and situations.

Reflection Questions — Plant New Seeds:

- What situations or emotional tones affect you most deeply, and how might these sensitivities reflect your Essential Nature rather than a flaw?

- Where in your life do your boundaries feel either too porous or too rigid, and what would a firm—but still permeable—boundary look like right now?

- Who are your nourishing "pollinators" that could respond with support if you allowed yourself to ask, and what small adjustment could help you protect your energy while staying open to mutual support and connection?

CONCLUSION:

Grow and Thrive

"Nature is always hinting at us. It hints over and over again. And suddenly we take the hint."

— Robert Frost

"The strongest oak of the forest is not the one that is protected from the storm and hidden from the sun. It's the one that stands in the open where it is compelled to struggle for its existence against the winds and rains and the scorching sun."

— Napoleon Hill

Whether we grow houseplants, cultivate outdoor gardens, or simply admire plants wherever we encounter them, we know, instinctively, that plants are as varied as the insects and animals of the world. When we notice a plant in our home or garden is failing to thrive, the nearly universal response is, "I wonder what it needs." If we encounter a tree that has a twisted limb, damage to its trunk, or is not growing full and tall, we may ponder, "I wonder what happened to it that compromised its growth."

Never, ever is our first thought, "It's not trying hard enough."

We don't blame plants for failing to thrive. We question their environment. Avid gardeners know that you can't plant a full sun plant in the shade and expect it to look like the picture on the plant tag. We know that leaving tender plants outside in freezing weather will kill them.

All these things are obvious when we look at the nature around us. Yet we often use an entirely different set of standards when we examine our own ability to grow and be healthy.

Humans *are* nature. Yes, we have a thinking brain, and we can reason. That is usually the vaulted hallmark of being human—the executive brain, the power of logic and thought. Yet we have put so much focus on how we are more evolved than other creatures that we believe that is the full story of being human. But the foundation of being healthy and productive and thriving as a person is the same as any other mammal. And any plant.

We need to plant ourselves in a climate where we feel a sense of belonging, one that feels aligned with our inner being and the ways in which we can truly take up the space we were meant to.

When we can tune in to our own Essential Nature and recognize that we need something unique to us—and different from anyone else in our lives—we will truly have the ability to grow to our full potential, to the height and width that is on our own unique plant tag.

I believe we knew, once, what we truly wanted. We gravitate toward it before the world steps in with its messages in the form of judgements and comparisons. Just as I went directly to nature as a child, we all had a time when we lived by instinct. We knew what we wanted to eat, or what color we liked, or which person in our lives made us feel safe. We all had some fascination, whether it be nature, like me, or music or machines or sports or butterflies.

But somewhere along the way, there was a judgment. Your laugh sounds weird. Your interest in geography or insects or car engines is nerdy and dumb. You should learn to throw a baseball instead of playing the violin. You should be smarter, funnier, prettier, stronger.

Yet all those attributes and interests and quirks make you *you*. No one can be a better you than you! And what you love and want and need to thrive is your unique, one-and-only Essential Nature. It was born into you, and it was tempered—for better and for worse—by experiencing the world.

When we can reconnect with that original version of ourselves—the one we didn't question because we didn't know we were supposed to—that's the key to finding fulfillment, to living as our true selves. Once we do this, it really is like a plant that is finally where it needs to be: It grows full, it flowers in the way it is meant to, it has a symbiotic relationship with its environment, it finds strength in rest, and it knows how to stand strong against life's challenges.

So dare to live by the words on your own unique plant tag—your size, zone, your flower season, and color. That is what makes you the exact human you are.

Imagine if we grew gardens to reflect the narratives of our society. All the flowers would be the same color, the same height, would never stop flowering, and would be perfect every day. In nature, that garden would never survive. Nature's strength—the very survival of species—lies in uniqueness, diversity, community, and symbiosis.

One of the most important plants in any landscape is the *focal plant*. It has at least one amazing characteristic that makes it the central point of interest—the most striking aspect—of the garden.

Be the focal plant in the garden of your life. Live like the amazing, resilient, vibrant being that you are.

ACKNOWLEDGEMENTS

If I were a plant, I would definitely be self-pollinating by nature, so writing this book challenged me. Because while writing itself is solitary, bringing a fully-formed book into the world is definitely not. It takes a willingness to find sources of support at every stage of growth. I am humbled and grateful to the people who offered consistent encouragement and enthusiasm for each small accomplishment.

First, I want to thank Dakota at Wandering Words media. She was the perfect combination of practical and gentle, which was so important for my first experience with editing. While I wanted to weep at times, it was a much better book after I accepted (most of) her strikethroughs and suggestions. And my appreciation to my coach, Ali, at selfpublishing.com. (I asked *a lot* of questions.) Thank you for celebrating each milestone with me.

Humble and heartfelt gratitude to Dr. Anthony Fredericks, a kindred soul in my love of nature. When I took the nerve-wracking step to send him a request for a review of my book—my first request to an accomplished and prolific author—his positive response and zeal for my manuscript expanded my heart (and my confidence).

To my true-blue pollinators, my believers-from-the-beginning and my enthusiastic supporters: Carol, Julie, Kim, Mindy, MJ, Phyllis, Madelyn, Christine, Kasey, and Samantha. You don't truly know how much your love and support has touched me. Whether you read the first draft, checked in out of the blue to encourage me, reached out to bookstore owners unbidden, or simply listened to me drone on about the human attributes of my beloved plants, you are the most beautiful flowers in the garden of my life. (If I've forgotten to mention anyone, I know I will remember you in the middle of the night after this has gone to press. If this happens, I'll make up for it in the acknowledgments of my *next* book.)

Sincere gratitude to my sister, Barb, for her lovely artwork. This book would not be what it is without her hours of work and the care she took to create both accurate and beautiful renderings of nature. Thank you for the labor of love. And thank God Mom and Dad had one more kid after me. Where would I be without you?

Love and true appreciation to my husband, Michael, who supports every single idea I've concocted, no matter how cockamamie, including deciding to finally share with the world how to live like a plant. I can have my head in the clouds because he never fails to hold onto the ropes of the balloon. He's my constant.

And finally, to all the clients I've worked with throughout my long career: Allowing me to share both your heartbreaks and your triumphs has been one of the most humbling and gratifying aspects of my life. This book has grown from the soil of our work together. It is a gift to you and to anyone who has ever doubted the beauty of their existence.

Moonflower (Datura)

The moonflower opens at night, its white, trumpet-shaped blooms glowing softly in the dark. Its rich scent calls in night-flying pollinators—doing vital work while the world sleeps.

Much of its importance goes unseen. Yet for certain species, the moonflower is essential.

Some of the most meaningful work happens quietly. Your gifts are just as beautiful, even if not everyone sees them.

ABOUT THE AUTHOR

Mary Rothwell is a licensed therapist, certified forest therapy practioner and lifelong observer of human and plant behavior. One of her life blessings was a long career working with young adults both in public schools and in college student mental health. Her roles included both clinician and administrator at HACC in Central Pennsylvania and at The Pennsylvania State University.

She currently hosts the podcast No Shrinking Violets and offers keynotes, staff training, and coaching for higher education and non-profit professionals as owner of Veria Consulting.

In addition to being a plant geek, writer, and speaker, Mary is a lover of trails seldom traveled and minion to cats. Her best days are spent with a book, a new recipe, or her favorite person. She can usually be found wandering through the woods or the streets of her beautiful city, scoping out the best coffeshops during her travels, or hitting the movie theater solo for late run showings, hoping she can be alone with her popcorn.

She lives in Central Pennsylvania with her husband, Mike, and their three geriatric cats, Clemson, Rigby and Sunny.

ARE YOU WILLING TO LEAVE A REVIEW?

Thank You For Reading My Book!

The world of books has changed tremendously since the days when my mom took my sister and me to the Bookmobile—a traveling library that came to our small town. Now, thanks to ebooks and online sellers, an entire world is at our fingertips!

While this is amazing for the love of books, it can make it hard for new authors to stand out and be found by those that would love and benefit from their writings.

Ratings and reviews raise the visibility, especially for those that self-publish. Leaving an honest review will help people find my book *and* make the next version of this book (and my future books) better!

Please take two minutes now to leave a helpful review on Amazon, letting me know what you thought of the book.

Thank you, sincerely,

Mary

maryrothwell.net/natureknows